## Praise for *Learner-Centered Leadership*

Parents across America drop their children off at public schools every day that look, operate, and educate in pretty much the same way their own schools did when they themselves were children. In his book, Devin lays out a roadmap to fundamentally reimagine public education for the children of today and tomorrow.

*Ben Austin, executive director, Kids Coalition*

Thank you to Devin Vodicka for this tremendous and timely contribution. We must rethink how we educate students, so *all* can have the opportunity to engage in extraordinary and equitable learning environments. None of this can happen without strong and visionary leadership. *Learner-Centered Leadership* provides grounded and practical guidance for thinking and leading differently.

*Jeff Wetzler, co-founder, Transcend*

Devin Vodicka's book is an urgent plea for us not to educate every student, but each student. Our strategies must embrace each student's individual story and meet each student's needs. Success is when each student is seen, valued, and educated.

*Caprice Young, EdD, national superintendent, Learn4Life*

Building on decades of work in learner-centered environments, Devin shares lessons learned and purpose-driven strategies that empower leaders to reach their fullest potential. This book is for any leader committed to helping every young person thrive.

*Emily Liebtag, executive director, Boundless*

Changing systems is messy work, but this book provides the inspiration and tools needed to truly transform schools to become learner-centered. With snapshots of success, frameworks for change, and clear steps to take along your journey, this book will empower any educator, anywhere, to make change a reality at your school.

 Dr. Jennifer Pieratt, president and founder of CraftED Curriculum

We have been waiting too long for a book that elegantly and powerfully transforms the term "learner-centered" to be something more than just a catchphrase. Dr. Vodicka has thoughtfully woven evidence, practice, and a compelling narrative to show what is possible when we lean in as leaders to create truly learner-centered systems. This book has important implications for schools across the globe that care about transforming the educational experience for all learners.

 Alan J. Daly, professor, University of California, San Diego

In *Learner-Centered Leadership*, Devin shares coherent strategic pathways to creating environments that support learners who develop agency and the capability to influence their communities and the world. This is the core of learning for life. *Learner-Centered Leadership* is a fabulous resource and well worth the read!

 Pamela Moran, retired superintendent
and co-author of *Timeless Learning*

An inspiring book by a visionary and courageous leader, *Learner-Centered Leadership* sends a compelling message: education must change to meet the needs of our children. More important, with rich and skillfully told stories of innovations on the ground, the book not only demonstrates that learner-centered education can happen but also provides practical guidance for how to make education learner-centered.

 Yong Zhao, author of *World Class Learners*

From superintendent's seat to the heart of Silicon Valley, Devin Vodicka has decades of leadership that have created a more "learner-centered" future. This book is filled with the stories and strategies that teach us how to make school more engaging and unlock the potential of students.

Brian Greenberg, CEO, the Silicon Schools Fund

*Learner-Centered Leadership* is an essential reference and resource for thoughtfully planning and leading the paradigm shift of putting the learner at the center of all we do in public education, which is essential if we are to truly engage every student. The book is soundly grounded in Dr. Vodicka's direct experiences both in leading change as an award-winning superintendent and supporting change in numerous districts as a consulting partner.

Brent McKim, president, National Council<br>of Urban Education Associations

Systemic change requires bold decision-making. It takes painting a vision of what's possible and charting a course to reach the new destination. With accelerating change a foundational component of today's paradigm, we must empower students to own their learning so that they can be successful far beyond graduation. *Learner-Centered Leadership* provides a research-based, experientially grounded framework for educational leaders to effectively empower their communities to reimagine what is possible for each learner, while developing a course of action to make it happen.

Thomas C. Murray, director of Innovation,<br>Future Ready Schools, Washington, DC

Devin has represented the learner experience throughout his extensive career, and now we get to see inside the great mind of this great leader. There is no better time than now to have access to a book focused on personalizing learning experiences around learner needs. I look forward to seeing the impact this book has on evoking transformative practices in classrooms around the globe.

Dr. Kecia Ray, CEO, K20Connect, LLC

Can public education be saved? Dr. Vodicka, author of *Learner-Centered Leadership*, not only says yes it can, he demonstrates how educational leaders must act now to do so. This book is a timely guide for teacher leaders, site administrators, and district office leaders who want to shift their thinking and their actions from a teacher-centered environment to a student-centered, equitable learning environment. Can we redesign public schools to be meaningful, relevant, interactive, engaging, future-focused, student-centered, learning-focused systems? The author describes the future by giving examples of these schools that actually exist today.

Delores B. Lindsey, co-founder, Center for<br>Culturally Proficient Educational Practice

In a rapidly changing world, there is no greater need than to have leaders who can create the conditions for learning. In *Learner-Centered Leadership*, Devin shares a blueprint for not only how to create a vision that everyone can buy into but how to build trust, relationships, and capacity to enable all learners to reach their full potential. This book is a must-read for all educators committed to creating schools that unleash the potential of all individuals.

Katie Martin, author of *Learner-Centered Innovation* and<br>VP of Leadership and Learning at Altitude Learning

Design, development, and sustainability of learner-centered school environments is critical for ensuring a productive future for each of our young people, and doing so requires skilled and steady leadership. Who better to explain how than Dr. Devin Vodicka?

Karen Cator, president and CEO, Digital Promise

A visionary and effective education leader, Vodicka draws on his own experience as well as research and frameworks from the private sector and cognitive and social science to provide a blueprint for how to become a learner-centered leader—regardless of your role in K-12 education. With wisdom and humility, he translates education and management buzzwords into meaningful, actionable terms; communicates guiding principles and questions to help educators navigate complexity and remain focused and adaptive as leaders; and issues an inspiring call to action to truly put student learning—and students as active contributors in their own learning—at the center of all efforts to transform education to meet the needs of the future, and most importantly of *all* of our children.

Beth Battle Anderson, executive director, Hill Learning Center

The hardest part of real change may well be leading its implementation. Here, Dr. Vodicka gives us a candid, insightful recounting of change-in-action by one of the earliest adopters of learner-centered learning, Vista Unified. It is an important read for education policymakers, administrators, and school boards around the country and the world.

Gerri Burton, New Learning Ventures

# LEARNER-CENTERED LEADERSHIP

# LEARNER-CENTERED LEADERSHIP

A Blueprint for Transformational Change in Learning Communities

**DEVIN VODICKA**

*Learner-Centered Leadership: A Blueprint for Transformational Change in Learning Communities*
© 2020 Devin Vodicka

All rights reserved. No part of this publication may be reproduced in any form or by any electronic or mechanical means, including information storage and retrieval systems, without permission in writing by the publisher, except by a reviewer who may quote brief passages in a review. For information regarding permission, contact the publisher at books@impress.org.

This book is available at special discounts when purchased in quantity for use as premiums, promotions, fundraisers, or for educational use. For inquiries and details, contact the publisher at books@impress.org.

Published by IMpress,
ImpressBooks.org, a division of Dave Burgess Consulting, Inc.
San Diego, CA
DaveBurgessConsulting.com

Library of Congress Control Number: 2020932471

Paperback ISBN: 978-1-948334-26-6

Ebook ISBN: 978-1-948334-27-3

Editing and book production by Reading List Editorial
Cover design by Kachergis Book Design
Interior design by Andrea Reider

# CONTENTS

Foreword: What Is a Learner-Centered Education? And Why the Need for a Shift? .............................. xiii
    *by Colleen Broderick*

Introduction ................................................. 1

CHAPTER 1: Making a Movement: What Happened at Vista .... 15

CHAPTER 2: A Framework for the Future .................... 41

CHAPTER 3: From Learner-Centered Education to Leadership .. 59

CHAPTER 4: A System for Breakthrough ..................... 83

CHAPTER 5: The Learner Takes Charge ..................... 105

CHAPTER 6: Managing Change, Changing Management ...... 133

CHAPTER 7: Accelerating Change .......................... 149

CHAPTER 8: The Future ................................... 159

Acknowledgments .......................................... 171

About the Author .......................................... 175

# FOREWORD: WHAT IS A LEARNER-CENTERED EDUCATION? AND WHY THE NEED FOR A SHIFT?

Colleen Broderick, Director of Learning at the International School of Zug and Luzern

When asked to define learner-centered education, I look to my grandmother. She taught in a community school in rural central New York State. I imagine it the stuff of old movies: the young woman charged with educating the community's children in a one-room schoolhouse, regardless of age or perceived ability.

In order to address the diversity of needs across all the students, collaboration and trust must have been essential. It was imperative that Grandmother create an environment where she and the students committed to one another. Rather than working independently, they needed to work in support of each other. That required a particular mindset about teaching, a special way of considering the relationship between teacher and student, of the way in which the learning environment was structured, and the nature of the curriculum. At its center, it required her to know and to partner with each learner.

For much of the twentieth century, schools got bigger, not smaller. And there were good reasons for that, like reducing costs and making greater use of diverse teacher expertise. Along with this change, however, the dynamics of education shifted. The conditions that necessitated a collaborative learning culture in the one-room schoolhouse gave way to standardization and efficiency.

Today, there is a new urgency. Given the accelerating pace of change in the world and the crushing amount of knowledge that is readily accessible, the tool kit that students need to develop now is very different than it used to be. Education today requires a very different commitment to children, one that expands beyond academic achievement. It requires a distinct departure from routine, standardized teaching and a shift toward a whole-child approach that honors each learner as unique. It requires the development of all parts of a child within a supportive and adaptive learning environment that values both social-emotional and academic growth in equal measure.

The ultimate goal of whole-child education is to empower students as creative, resilient, inquiry-driven citizens who are able to self-advocate, develop strong relationships, navigate complex information, and drive their own learning in diverse environments beyond the classroom. These outcomes, complex and nuanced, require a shift toward learner-centered education.

There is no doubt that delivering on a more robust set of outcomes is simply more complicated. Today, however, we find ourselves in a Goldilocks moment: conditions are "just right" to place learners at the center, empowering them to be the primary agents of their learning journey. Both our growing understanding of cognitive and psychological development and the ability to intentionally integrate technology have made it possible to responsibly put the learner in the driver's seat.

# FOREWORD

I know from my grandmother's experience that learner-centered education is not new to education. Instead, it is a shift to embrace a powerful pedagogy that has been developing over the past hundred years, enabling us to act on what we know about how human beings learn. Learning theories such as progressivism, situated learning, constructivism, competency-based and experiential learning are foundational to learner-centered models.

What binds these theories together are principles that are intended to deal holistically with learners in the context of real-world learning situations. The principles center around empowering the learner to construct meaning from experience, to generate and pursue personally relevant goals, to create and use a repertoire of thinking and reasoning strategies that include thinking about thinking, and to engage in social interactions that require diverse mediums of communication with others.

To tackle what's best for learners will require real change, not just a new to-do list of activities or additions to the already full plates that exist for school administrators and classroom educators. As Will Richardson points out, "Change in schools is not really about teaching. It's not even about education. It's about learning."

In brief, learner-centered education is a mindset that stems from the belief that every learner is unique and capable. It's a philosophy that recognizes that all decisions must measure up to the question "What is best for learners?"

# INTRODUCTION

It's time for the education establishment to acknowledge that the world is changing too quickly and too completely to know, today, what every student should learn for tomorrow. It's changed so much that even the notion of *all students* seems too reductive and liable to erase the experiences, interests, and potential of too many students. It's time to find an education that can respond to *each* student. A truly learner-centered education. Let me give you an example.

Each time I walked through Rancho Buena Vista High School, Diego (not his real name) had the biggest and most contagious grin. "Remember me?" he joked. At the time of this story, I was the superintendent to a school district of twenty-five thousand students, making a school visit, but Diego and I first met each other a decade before when I was an elementary school principal.

Over the years, I'd formed a fairly fixed and two-dimensional image of Diego: I assumed that he had become a happy, hard-working young man, just like the happy, hard-working kid he'd been back in the first grade. Then one afternoon I arrived at work to find an urgent message to contact Diego's mother. Over the course of the next hour, I was forced to rethink all of my assumptions.

I quickly learned that Diego's family had been in a desperate situation for some time. His father died when he was in middle school, and his mother had worked two jobs to support the family ever since.

## INTRODUCTION

That is, until recently, when she fell ill. Consequently, Diego had taken over trying to support the family, working forty hours a week while also trying to finish high school. He often worked late into the night to avoid missing his classes. And it was taking a huge toll. Not only was he falling behind in school and at risk of not graduating, but despite his hard work, the bills were falling behind, too. At this point, his family couldn't pay their rent.

Diego's mother is strong, and proud, and not comfortable asking for help. But throughout our tearful discussion, I learned that Diego's lifelong dream had been to graduate high school and be the first in his family to attend college. He had followed the rules, worked tirelessly, and as a result, he should have been just months away from achieving his dream. But now his mother was watching it all slip away, and she didn't know how to stop it.

By this point, I was already deeply moved and ready to do just about anything to help this family. What she said next will stay with me forever.

She said she contacted me because of something Diego told her over the years: that I smiled at him. That's it. Smiling. Apparently, that was unusual for Diego. So much so that this incredible young man would go home from school and tell his mom about me, that his principal, and later superintendent, smiled and sometimes talked to him.

The next morning after hearing of his troubles, I went straight to Diego's school and pulled him out of class. I asked how I could help, and he begrudgingly admitted that he could use some clean clothes and school supplies. I discovered that his teachers were deducting points from his grades because he was not bringing basic materials, like pencils or paper. I had to press him to talk more deeply about graduation. It was only then that I noticed, for the first time ever, that Diego seemed deflated. He said he didn't know how he could possibly catch up and graduate, and that he was just taking things

INTRODUCTION

day by day. More than anything, he said, he was worried about disappointing his mother.

How could this have happened? How could we not have been aware of his family's urgent need for assistance? How could we not have noticed that this student, who had been "on track" for years, was in big trouble? How could we instead interpret his behavior as not trying hard enough, when the exact opposite was true? I know what I saw. I saw a diligent young person trying to persevere and succeed despite very difficult circumstances. Instead, Diego had "slipped through the cracks." I was heartbroken.

Fortunately, we caught our mistake in time. Once we became aware of the challenges Diego was facing, everything changed. From teachers to staff to business partners, our community came together to help. Thanks to a number of partnerships we'd developed with community agencies, Diego received clean clothes and school supplies. He was so grateful you would think we'd given him the moon instead of T-shirts and number 2 pencils. Others donated gift cards for grocery stores so that he and his mom could have food. An innovative grant program for families at risk of becoming homeless helped us to secure emergency rent payments for three months.

At school, the staff formed a comprehensive plan to get Diego back on track to graduate. The counselors became engaged in his success, and even the principal implemented a weekly process to monitor his progress. Academic interventions were launched, including extended-day blended-learning courses to help remediate credit deficiencies. Our district-wide college readiness specialist visited Diego's home, working alongside him to ensure he had a clear pathway to attend a local community college after graduation.

Suddenly, instead of the system—me, as superintendent, the principal, the school staff—assuming that Diego was on track, we were responding to his actual needs. Now, instead of seeing him as

## INTRODUCTION

a student struggling to conform to a system, we saw him as an individual with unique needs. Our team members became resourceful advocates and partners in Diego's journey, orienting and adapting to direct our collective efforts with a clear focus on the learner. A couple of months later, I received a message from Diego: "Hey, I have good news . . . I will be the first person in my family to go to college!"

Diego made it. He worked hard and earned his diploma. When he needed help, assistance was available so that he could achieve his dream. By completing high school and going to college, he will have a better chance to gain meaningful employment in the future. I have no doubt that he will be successful. This is a story with a happy ending.

But we can also imagine a different scenario here, one that plays out every day in schools around the country. Diego could have easily dropped out of high school to focus full-time on jobs that helped him to pay the bills. We can imagine that in his situation, it may have been tempting to try to take a shortcut to get ahead. We can predict that his entire life would likely have been more difficult, more of an uphill struggle, if he had not completed his high school education.

Diego's story is that of just one student whose needs weren't being met—or seen. But it's far from unique among the fifty-five million children in our nation's public schools, a system that is working overtime to improve but is still falling behind. Almost 20 percent of students in the United States do not graduate from high school. The gap in the graduation rate between lower-income students and others is about 15 percent. African American and Latino students graduate at lower rates than white and Asian students. While there have been modest gains in the past few years, the overall results have been largely the same since the early 1970s.

The plateau in graduation rates is an example of how we have "optimized" our current system. Over the past several decades we have experienced many reforms, and there have been many well-intended efforts to improve our schools. Unfortunately, the result has

INTRODUCTION

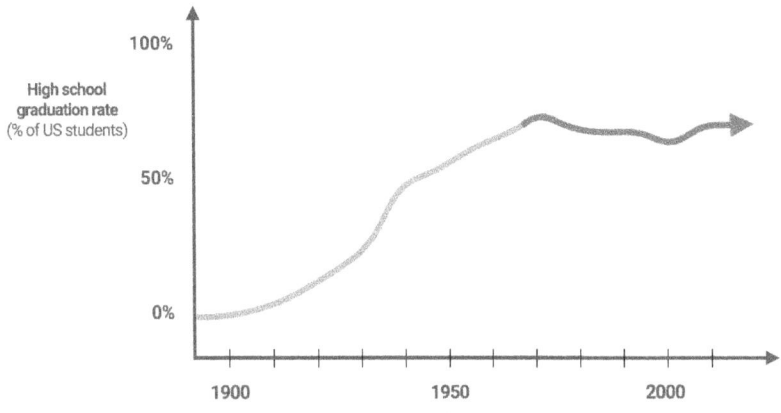

Source: EPE Research Center (2012), Murnane (2013)

often been akin to spinning a hamster wheel faster—lots of effort with very little real movement.

One of the reasons that we see so many students who do not complete their education is that students tend to become less engaged as they move from elementary to middle and then to high school. Any educator who has spent time visiting different classrooms has observed this phenomenon, and a significant student survey conducted by Gallup makes the trend painfully obvious.

So, we have to ask ourselves some questions about these outcomes. Why is the graduation rate stuck at around 80 percent? Why do students tend to become less engaged as they move through the system?

While there are many factors that legitimately contribute to this harsh reality, my experience has shown that an underappreciated and meaningful reason that many students disengage and drop out is due to the lack of acknowledgement of each student's uniqueness. As in Diego's case, that lack of acknowledgement of individuality causes educators to miss important things about a student, and this disconnection often causes students to disengage.

INTRODUCTION

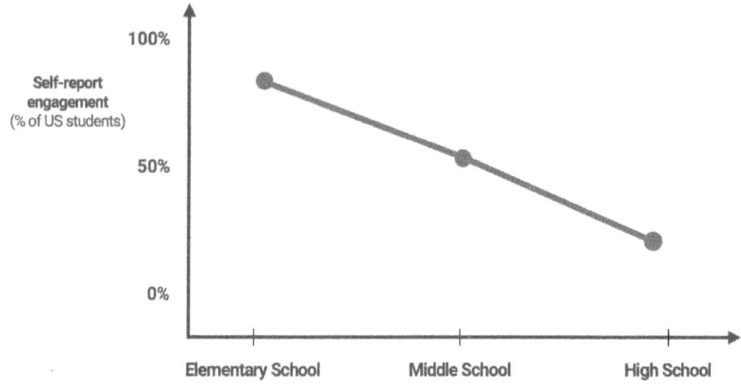

Source: The Gallup Student Poll (2013)

The inflexibility of education is a barrier to meaningful learning. Learners come to school with dramatically different levels of background knowledge and wide variance in the ways in which they advance in their understanding. Just about any elementary school teacher will tell you that they are generally attempting to meet a range of subject matter mastery that spans several grade levels, and secondary teachers see this range expand as students matriculate to the higher grades. The "teaching to the middle" strategy often results in some students feeling as if the pace is too fast, while others would prefer to accelerate at a greater rate, with very few, if any, feeling that it's just right.

Given the fact that our students are often disconnected and compelled to comply with an inflexible system that continues to treat all learners as if they are the same, I am amazed with how many of our kids persist.

Diego persisted. In spite of his sense that he was invisible and in spite of being penalized for missing homework and assignments, he continued to show up. He continued to make his best effort to succeed. After more than two decades of working with learners, I can confidently state that while he is an exceptional young man, his story

## INTRODUCTION

is illustrative of the inspirational effort that we see from our learners each and every day.

If we can find better ways to connect and inspire every learner, our students, families, communities, and society will stand a much better chance to successfully navigate the monumental challenges and opportunities that are on the horizon. It is extremely urgent that we ensure *all* learners reach their potential.

Learner-centered education means co-constructing learning experiences in a way that respects and builds on the unique strengths, interests, and values of *each* learner. By employing this approach, we seek to shift not only the educational system but also society at large.

My perspective on this is driven by my own experience as a first-generation American who felt very different as a child of Czech and Dutch immigrants. Apart from my siblings, I was the only one who ate kolaches, celebrated a name day (a special day of the year to celebrate the saint for which you were named), and wore Czech clothes to school. In spite of my culture, I had the same experience of school as any of my classmates who brought different family and cultural customs with them. Because my teachers did not recognize my differences, I often felt that they did not see me. In retrospect, one could say that there was an expectation to conform to institutional norms. I could fit in at school by letting go of my family identity, or I could stand out at school by embracing my uniqueness.

I didn't look dissimilar from my classmates—I was a white kid at a predominantly white school with predominantly white teachers. But inside I felt different from those around me. In addition to how culture shapes the educational experiences of students like me, I should be clear that race, racism, and structural racism have profound effects for many students of color. As a white man, I can only imagine and sympathize with how race influences the experience of others.

By embracing and celebrating the unique strengths of every learner, it is my hope that we can begin to see all forms of difference,

INTRODUCTION

including cultural and racial diversity, as the assets they truly are. Being learner-centered, therefore, is a direct challenge to inequality in all forms. In the same ways that we want schools to be learner-centered, society should be human-centered. At its essence, learner-centered education and human-centered societal mindsets embrace the notion that equity requires us to see and know one another as real people and then to design improvements as a community.

Brent McKim, the president of the Jefferson County Teachers Association in Louisville, Kentucky, drew a visual at a recent convening that illustrates how a learner-centered approach is part of a broader human-centered paradigm. It is my belief that education has an enduring impact in establishing habits and perspectives that our students carry forward throughout their lives. If we begin with education, we can affect broader change throughout society over

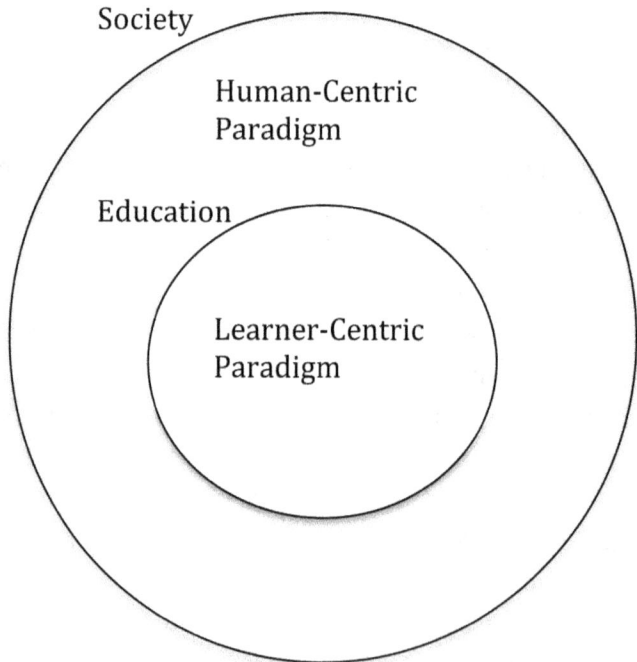

## INTRODUCTION

an extended period of time. Being learner-centered is a radical and potentially revolutionary approach that holds the potential to eradicate inequality in all forms, including classism, racism, ageism, and sexism. And it begins by simply seeing one another.

### Our Students Are Unique

Our communities are increasingly diverse, and we are also gaining more awareness about the different ways our brains may be wired, also known as *neurodiversity*. But our system remains unflinchingly entrenched in the factory-model origins that gave rise to it during the dawn of the industrial age. In this factory-model approach, just as workers were referred to as "hands" who were expected to be proficient with repetitive tasks, our students are implicitly asked to check their identities at the door and to become compliant with adult-directed activities.

The lack of recognition for the humanity and individuality of our students is one of the reasons that so many of them disengage from learning. They feel that they are not valued as individuals. They feel invisible. While Diego had great respect for his teachers, he did not feel that he had a connection with them, and consequently he did not share his situation. Sadly, the hard-working, well-intentioned team of educators working with him were blind to the reality of his challenges.

Diego and I felt unseen as students. For Diego, it was the feeling that no one knew, or cared, that his family was struggling to survive and that he had been expected to take on the heavy responsibilities of an adult even while trying to keep up with school. For me, it was the lack of recognition that the culture of my family was different from mainstream American culture, which led me to feel disconnected. When I've asked educators to estimate the percentage of students that are from immigrant families, most are surprised to learn that one in four are first- or second-generation Americans. How are we recognizing and celebrating diversity in our schools? It is unlikely

INTRODUCTION

that a standardized approach will anticipate and incorporate the cultural diversity that exists in our classrooms, our schools, and in our communities.

## The Student's World Is Complex

In addition to the cultural disconnect that can lead us to disregard the unique backgrounds of our learners, we tend to cling to this idea that we can somehow "teach to the middle" and achieve educational success. This approach prioritizes efficiencies in the delivery of instruction over the varied needs of the learners. In addition to the common-sense knowledge that different people learn in different ways and at different rates, emerging research is revealing that in fact we are all "jagged" individuals, and that we need to embrace what education theorist Todd Rose calls "the end of average."

> It's so ubiquitous that it's hard to see.
>
> We design textbooks to be age-appropriate, but that means, what does the average kid of this age know and can do? Textbooks that are designed for the average will be a pretty bad fit for most kids.
>
> Then you think of things like the lockstep, grade-based organization of kids, and you end up sitting in a class for a fixed amount of time and get a one-dimensional rating in the form of a grade, and a one-dimensional standardized assessment.[1]

The rigidity of our industrial-era approach in education stands in stark contrast with the dynamism outside of schools. As

---

[1] Todd Rose, "Standards, Grades and Tests Are Wildly Outdated," interview with Anya Kamenetz, *nprED*, NPR online, February 16, 2016, https://www.npr.org/sections/ed/2016/02/16/465753501/standards-grades-and-tests-are-wildly-outdated-argues-end-of-average.

## INTRODUCTION

educators, we must also recognize the accelerating pace of change in the rest of the world. In the 1970s, Gordon Moore, the cofounder and former chairman of Intel, made an observation, now known as "Moore's Law," that computing power doubles roughly every two years. This has held true for decades, where rapidly advancing technology is creating new and disruptive possibilities at a faster and faster pace. Voice recognition software as we know and use it today, for example, was science fiction only a decade ago. Now this technology is ubiquitous. Our phones come with Siri and Google Assistant, and our homes rely on Alexa. Soon drive-through workers and customer service call centers will be outsourced to automated bots using these rapidly advancing technologies. This is just the tip of the iceberg. We are now at the beginning of exponential changes that are at the same time enabling incredible global connectedness and collaboration and also eliminating entire occupations at rapid speeds. I now spend much of my time in the heart of the Silicon Valley. I have daily conversations with leaders who have switched to "virtual assistants," which are essentially artificial intelligence bots that assist with everything from scheduling meetings to purchasing gifts for family members. Monopolies such as the US Postal Service are going through massive downsizing as new technologies have led to the near elimination of letters and other physical mailings. Disintermediation has completely disrupted entire industries, such as music and entertainment, where we have gone from record stores and movie rental outlets to on-demand streaming services.

All of these forces are giving rise to the "gig economy," where workers are often earning revenue from multiple sources without being classified as an employee by any of them. The days of spending an entire career with one company disappeared with my parents' generation. Now the days of spending even a single day with one company might be eliminated in mine. It is hard to imagine what my children will experience. It is even harder to imagine that they will have a "manager" who tells them what to do, when to do it, and how to do it.

INTRODUCTION

## World Economic Forum 2022 Skills Outlook

| Growing | Declining |
|---|---|
| 1. Analytical thinking and innovation | 1. Manual dexterity, endurance, and precision |
| 2. Active learning and learning strategies | 2. Memory, verbal, auditory, and spatial abilities |
| 3. Creativity, originality, and initiative | 3. Management of financial, material resources |
| 4. Technology design and programming | 4. Technology installation and maintenance |
| 5. Critical thinking and analysis | 5. Reading, writing, math, and active listening |
| 6. Complex problem-solving | |
| 7. Leadership and social influence | 6. Management of personnel |
| | 7. Quality control and safety awareness |
| 8. Emotional intelligence | |
| 9. Reasoning, problem-solving, and ideation | 8. Coordination and time management |
| | 9. Visual, auditory, and speech abilities |
| 10. Systems analysis and evaluation | |
| | 10. Technology use, monitoring, and control |

Source: Future of Jobs Report 2018, World Economic Forum

And yet, most schools are organized to prepare students for a world that no longer exists. The gap between what we do in most classrooms and what our kids need is so striking that some believe it may already be too late. Data from Gallup surveys shows that

## INTRODUCTION

Americans' confidence in public schools has dropped to half of what it was thirty years ago.[2]

I recently had a reporter ask me if I felt like I was "wasting time" on the lost cause of public education. While I pride myself on being a calm and steady person, I took great offense to that statement. In spite of the challenges, I believe that there is great reason to be optimistic. Just as our community rallied around Diego, I have seen communities of extremely dedicated and caring individuals push themselves to find creative solutions that address the complex challenges of our time.

I have seen significant, positive change made by educators who work to reshape the system to meet the needs of their students, and not the reverse. As a result, I have exceptional confidence in our collective capacity to create and scale a postindustrial model of education that better serves our students, our families, our communities, and our future. The foundation of my optimism is our children. I see incredible resilience in young people like Diego. I believe that one of the opportunities we have dramatically overlooked in education is to see our children as active contributors in their learning.

If we implement this change in perspective well, it will result in an education that is improved in quality as well as in terms of flexibility. We are now in an era where learners can be at the center of their experience. An age in which we can recognize and celebrate the uniqueness and individuality of every child. It is time for us to move away from efficiencies that are good for adults. Time for us to be oriented to effectiveness. Time for us to be aligned with the needs of the modern world. It is time for us to be learner-centered.

---

[2]Jeffrey M. Jones, "Confidence in US Public Schools at New Low," *Gallup News*, June 20, 2012, Politics, https://news.gallup.com/poll/155258/confidence-public-schools-new-low.aspx.

INTRODUCTION

## **KEY QUESTIONS**

- How might we ensure that all students are connected and supported in their learning?
- How might we reverse the "engagement dip" that we see as learners move through grade levels?
- How might we better recognize and celebrate the diversity of our learners, our families, and our communities?
- How might we reduce the gap between the pace of change within schools and the pace of change in the world around us?

Please use the hashtag #LCLeadership and share your responses on social media.

# 1

# MAKING A MOVEMENT: WHAT HAPPENED AT VISTA

### The Student Takes Charge

As the new superintendent of Vista Unified School District, when I spoke of the need to have a strategic plan, I was greeted with what seemed like an allergic reaction from everyone I talked to. But in the end, seeking input from stakeholders to inform our strategic plan became one of the most profoundly impactful experiences of my career.

I understood why these other stakeholders were so wary about what needed to be done: previous disappointments with complicated plans had ended up wasting time and energy, often "sitting on the shelf" at their conclusion and not resulting in any real change. To distance this strategic plan from its problematic predecessors, one of my savvy board members suggested that I use a different term: we settled on calling our plan the "Blueprint for Educational Excellence and Innovation."

Following that blueprint theme would prove to be pivotal. I knew it would be important to get input from those who would be affected by the plan. I used the analogy of doing a home renovation and stressed how important it would be to have input from my wife and children before drawing up the plans and knocking out walls. With that in mind, I met with students, community leaders, families, school leaders, teachers, and classified staff members to conduct forums that would inform the development of the plan.

The student forums were the most powerful learning experience I have ever had. In many respects, I feel regretful that I waited so long in my career to hear the voices of students in such a meaningful way. If there is one strong recommendation that I share now with other leaders—one takeaway from this book if you read no further—it is that you should also take the time to listen to the learners. Taking the time to solicit input, and to act on it, is one of the best ways for leaders to model and create a learner-centric approach.

In the 2012–13 school year, I ended up holding more than sixty forums, and each successive interaction fueled new insights on my part and led me to seek even more understanding. I met with "high-achieving" students who told me that we had not done enough to prepare them to be independent after graduation. I met with students who were deemed "at-risk," students who were at our continuation high schools, and even groups of students who had dropped out of school. I asked them all to describe what they liked about school and what we should change. I asked who else I should meet with to get more input. One of the elements of each forum was to ask the students to write one word that described their school experience on a sheet of paper. At the conclusion of this series of forums, we put all of the student feedback into a word cloud that visualized their input.

The largest word at the center of the word cloud, the one that had been used most frequently, was "irrelevant."

## MAKING A MOVEMENT: WHAT HAPPENED AT VISTA

This discovery was like a bucket of cold water being thrown in my face. One colleague described it as a kick in the stomach. It was a wake-up call for me and for our team. How could we expect to succeed when our learners did not see the relevance in their educational experiences?

Fortunately, we had an abundance of additional input. I had brought a few other leaders into the forums, which I had begun on my own. We sat together and reflected on the conversations, asking ourselves what we had heard from the students about when they had felt engaged and inspired with their learning. The students mentioned that they had outside interests they wanted to connect to their learning. They wanted to have more choice and have the ability to move at their own rate. They wanted to engage in complex, real-world problem solving. They wanted to use digital resources (like the smart phones in their pockets) to expand their opportunities and their access to the world they were engaged in beyond school. What we were hearing is that they wanted learning to be personal. One student said it in a powerful way: "I don't want school to happen to me. I want to drive my own learning."

This led us to develop and implement a "blueprint" that I would characterize as a whole-child, learner-centered approach. In addition to plans around family and community engagement, social and emotional systems of support, and high-quality adaptive core curriculum, we had two strategies expressly devoted to personalized learning environments and personalized learning pathways.

I had no idea at the time that this commitment to a balanced, individualized learning model would create glimpses into the future of teaching and learning. We were just trying to listen and be responsive to our kids. As it turns out, that responsiveness to our learners is at the heart of a movement that holds the potential to be the new model of postindustrial education. We are now at the cusp of a potential transformation from mass production in schools to mass personalization.

During my five-year tenure as superintendent in Vista Unified School District, we implemented districtwide changes that resulted in major improvements across every academic and behavioral metric, from college readiness to chronic absenteeism. These improvements attracted national attention, resulting in recognitions and awards including a $10 million XQ Super School prize and visits to the White House. Now, as chief impact officer at Altitude Learning, I have the privilege of supporting educators around the country in our efforts to ensure that all students will have the opportunity to be empowered through whole-child, personalized learning. In this book, I will share reflections and ideas related to strategies and actions that leaders can take to set the conditions that will accelerate a collective shift into learner-centered education.

The journey to learner-centered education in Vista Unified began by listening to our students. Throughout this book, I will share reflections and ideas related to strategies and actions that leaders can take to set the conditions to accelerate a collective shift to learner-centered education.

## Postindustrial Models of Education

The World Economic Forum report *The Future of Jobs 2018* predicts that by 2025, the ratio of human to machine labor will shift to a majority of work being done by machines (including computing technology), with near-term declines in jobs available for assembly line work, data entry, and postal service clerks. The world has become increasingly postindustrial. It is naive to presume that public education will be immune to these changes.

But our schools still belong to the industrial era, the age of factories—both in their goals and their approach. In the postindustrial era, skills such as innovation and active learning will be increasingly valued, while many of the skills that have been emphasized in the factory model of teaching and learning will be less important. Like

> Paramount Unified School District in Los Angeles County is another great example of the power of a bias to action. Confronted with potential overcrowding at their comprehensive high school, their team came together and decided to open an innovative high school, Odyssey STEM Academy, that could serve as a catalyst for transformation. At Odyssey STEM Academy, learners have individual goals, customized lists of assignments, extensive hands-on learning experiences, opportunities for inquiry, interdisciplinary engagement, and anytime/anywhere immersive experiences in the community, including in work-based settings.
>
> Paramount is a school district where 94 percent of students are socioeconomically disadvantaged. They are not a particularly well-funded district, and they did not receive any special outside assistance to spark their changes. Quite simply, it was their community and the district leadership that had the will to act and an orientation to action that created expanded possibilities for their learners. Also critical in their story is the fact that they engaged learners in the design and development of the new school. This is another example of the power of reframing the role of our students to see them as active contributors and not as passive vessels of their education.

other industrial-age systems, school systems are designed as hierarchies, intended to have directives flow from the top of the org chart down to the line workers in a predictable, orderly fashion. These types of systems are designed for stability. They also tend to be organized around status, where managers dress in more formal attire, occupy corner offices, and rely on positional authority. The problem with this model is that it presumes a unidirectionality that is absent in actual reality.

It's like riding on a train. Trains can be a very efficient mode of transport, moving hundreds of people at once. However, the train will only go where there are tracks. The departure and arrival times are pre-established. Train passengers must conform to the system.

Now think about our schools. We have used railroad-like terms like "tracking" in the past. Our bells ring at consistent intervals like the arrivals and departures of trains. We provide a limited number of potential destinations for our passengers. Students are "on track" or "off track" for success. We have created a system of schools that looks and feels like a railroad experience for our students.

What we want for our learners in a postindustrial system of learning is for their experience to be like driving a car. Think of the experience of driving. We come and go when we want. We can take different routes. We have the autonomy to customize our vehicles to reflect our unique identities.

What if our educational system promoted learning as a driving experience for students? What if they had real choices in terms of when and how they learned? What if they actually had the ability to determine where they want to go? What if, instead of creating tracks, we set about to create numerous pathways for our students so that they could drive their own learning?

This would require us to approach teaching and learning in very different ways. But if we want to shift to a more personal model, one that recognizes the uniqueness of every child, we will need to embrace different pathways. We will also need to create new and different "rules of the road" to ensure safe travels. We will need to think about new ways to provide real-time feedback, akin to a GPS for learning, that can help guide the driver to their destination.

Creating this new system will not be easy. There are numerous challenges and barriers. But we are inventors. We are innovators. We must not be satisfied with a system that prepares students to be passengers instead of drivers, particularly when lifelong learning and the ability to navigate their own journey will be so critical in the era of adaptive change that is on the horizon.

Before digging into the "how" of creating a new system of learner-centered education, it is important to also recognize that there is emerging consensus about "what" our educational system can and should be in a postindustrial era.

## The Need for a Framework

"I know it when I see it."

That's what many educators and educational leaders will say when you ask them to describe the ideal learning experience. Unfortunately, our lack of ability to describe what we want impedes our ability to have conversations about how to design and create the conditions for meaningful learning.

In my training as an administrator, school leaders also went through a phase where we were taught to focus our teacher evaluation observations solely on what the teacher was doing. In this teacher-centric approach, the underlying sentiment was that we could only influence the behaviors of staff and should therefore not attend to the experience of the students in our evaluations of effectiveness. While it is true that there are many variables that impact student learning, this experience is symptomatic of a systemic approach that has focused on adults, in this case at the explicit exclusion of the students.

It is time for us to be focused on our learners and their learning, and then to work backward to redefine the role of an effective teacher. We need to shift away from *instructional* frameworks and focus on *learning* frameworks, especially as our world and our schools move further into the future.

## Ladder Versus Knot Learning

Some learning follows a relatively predictable and linear progression. I will refer to this as *ladder learning*, where a student proceeds from one rung on the ladder to the next. Learning can also take the form of much more complex, open-ended challenges and projects that have patterns in their resolution but more than one right answer. I will refer to this as *knot learning*, which represents the entanglement and irregular shapes that emerge from a series of knots.

Many of our efforts to use adaptive technology in education have focused on ladder learning. This type of learning can be achieved through computer-based programs that help to resolve issues of pace but tend to offer very little flexibility in terms of pathways. Ladder, learning systems usually have one right answer to a particular problem and generally are organized much like a series of progressively more difficult worksheets, which are automatically scored by digital technology, which then generates the next worksheet or assignment for the learner. These ladder-learning systems have been helpful in curricular areas that lend themselves to this approach, such as math facts and early literacy skills like letter and sound recognition.

Knot learning is a much more challenging problem and more accurately reflects the thinking we do in authentic problem-solving. Effective educators have been masterfully organizing project-based learning experiences for many years, inspired to do so by the incredible impacts they see in both academic development and social-emotional learning. Tackling real-world challenges also builds confidence and competence.

| Ladder Learning | Knot Learning |
| --- | --- |
| One right answer | Multiple possible answers |
| Linear progressions | Nonlinear progressions |
| Well-suited for screen-based, adaptive learning programs | Well-suited for group activities in authentic contexts |
| Individual | Social |
| Develops knowledge | Develops knowledge, habits, and skills |
| Academic | Academic and social-emotional |
| Can vary by pace | Can vary by pace and path |

## Empowering Students by Embracing Change

The ladder and knot models are analogues to the train tracks and the road systems. Just as our transportation system continues to evolve by building on the train system and by adding roads and highways, our educational system has an opportunity to take a massive evolutionary leap rather than continue to recreate what we have done in the past. We need to continue to find ways to accelerate progress on ladder learning by using adaptive learning technology, *and* we need to embrace the complexities of knot learning, where students are solving meaningful problems and are empowered to drive their own educational experiences.

There has been significant progress in the use of digital learning to catalyze progress with ladder learning, and we are also now on the cusp of being able to leverage technology as an accelerator for complex problem-solving and project-based learning. But teaching a student to solve a discrete math problem is a different task than asking a student to use math to resolve a complex social issue such as homelessness. Therefore, we need to be thoughtful in ensuring that learners will develop the capacity to make progress on both of these types of challenges.

## The Learner-Centered Classroom

This may all sound good in theory, but what does learner-centered education look like in a classroom? When students have the power to tackle real-world challenges *and* control their progress in ladder-learning experiences, it's no surprise that one sees a mix of individual, self-paced learning in those areas that lend themselves to more linear progressions, such as reading and math, with the remaining time focused on whole-class projects that emphasize collaboration, critical thinking, creativity, and communication. Reflection to promote self-awareness is a common thread in both ladder and knot

Classroom Snapshots: Vista Unified School District, 2016

modes. Individual needs, and therefore individual learning paths, vary based on the backgrounds and diverse needs of the learners.

For learners, this dual mode of personalization, which incorporates both path and pace, embraces individual progress and also promotes social development to build self-efficacy, collaboration, and problem-solving skills. Learner-centered systems ensure that learners are developing as individual contributors, while also impacting their local and global communities.

Consider Daniel's experience as a student at Vista High School. As we implemented our personal learning approach, his schedule changed from isolated classes to longer blocks with teams of teachers. They spent time with him, getting to know his strengths and interests, and quickly realized that he had a passion for computers. The team of teachers co-constructed a series of learning experiences that connected the academic standards with his area of interest, and he soon began to find that his curiosity about computers was helping him to improve in his reading and writing. He also began to see how computational thinking could help his performance in mathematics. He described this change as being like a light switch had gone on for him. Daniel emerged as a leader who said he saw a bright future for himself because he now knew that he enjoyed learning and growing.

Marla had a similar transformation at Vista High. For her, it was cooking that served as an inspiration for her studies. She had been thriving in the culinary arts program and struggling in academic areas, until her team of teachers tailored her assignments to build on her interest in cooking. She then produced well-researched cookbooks and also found that she enjoyed the design process as she worked to publish them. While her initial interest was cooking, she soon found herself enamored with graphic design and digital media. Her achievement in school also improved across the board as she began to see multiple pathways for success in the future.

As we expanded the implementation of "personal learning" across the school district, students throughout began to engage in challenging projects that focused on real-world challenges. While there was still a time and place for whole-class, teacher-led experiences, more and more of the time was being spent in small groups, which provided opportunities for collaboration and customization. Rows of desks gave way to flexible furniture, and students were more physically active and mobile. Learning began to extend outside of classrooms and into outdoor experiences. Students collaborated with one another as they discussed, debated, and engaged in dialogue on complex topics. In short, learner-centered is not independent study. If we are to focus on learners, we must begin with seeing them and knowing them. What follows is inevitably a more engaging, social experience.

As a result, the promise of learner-centered education is that *all* learners can be the best version of themselves *and* improve communities and society. It's time we move beyond the simplistic notions of learning and recognize that it is a "both/and" proposition that can better serve individual students and our collective society. It is time we lean into the complexities of the challenge. Our kids and our future depend on it.

## When Do We Give the Keys to the Learners?

My daughter is currently learning how to drive. Before we give her the car keys, she is required to go through a series of structured learning experiences, including structured lessons to learn about the rules of the road, watching safety videos, and working with a certified instructor. After all of those activities, she must take an exam to earn her learner's permit, at which point she can drive under the supervision of one of her parents. After months of such practice, she will be able to take a behind-the-wheel test to earn her provisional driver's license, which will allow her to drive herself and family members. If she can drive without incident for an entire year, she will then be allowed to drive friends who are under the age of eighteen.

In other words, we don't just give the keys to a new driver and say, "Go for it!" In an educational world where we want learners to drive their own experiences, we need to similarly scaffold their learning and set them up for success. At Altitude Learning, we think about this as a progression through an experiential learning cycle, which typically begins with teacher-led activities where the educator models and demonstrates the lesson. Next is a co-led experience, during which the educator and learner work side-by-side (much like the driving instructor who has a customized vehicle that enables them to take the wheel or brake when needed). Finally, the learner leads the experience, actually driving through their own planning, engagement, evaluation, and reflective understanding of their experience. Another way to describe this is that the learner needs to see the learning, then own the learning, and then drive the learning.

In the learner-centered model, these necessary scaffolds and supports provide the structure that is essential to accelerate learning for all. I believe in a human-centered approach to this model, with an ultimate aim of empowering the learner to enable the complete learning cycle, including self-understanding, planning, designing their own learning experiences, and

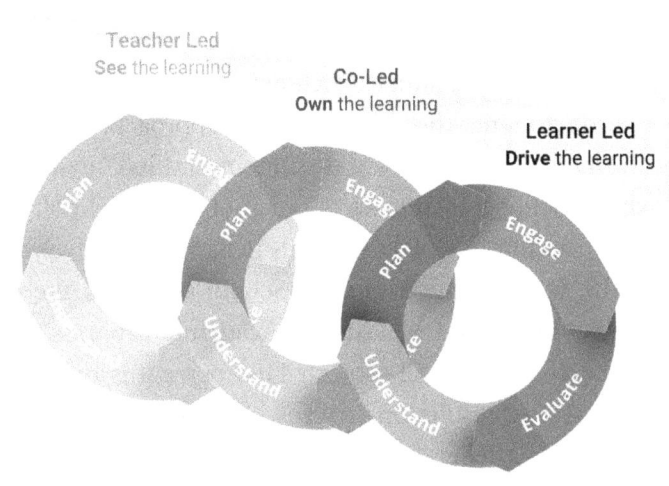

Altitude Learning Experiential-Learning Cycles

evaluating their progress. With that goal in mind, there are interlocking influences that are both required and helpful in creating the conditions for this learner empowerment.

In many schools, teachers currently are asked to serve as learning designers and are empowered to develop the experiences they feel are best suited to their learners. Given the scaffolds required to shift from teacher-led to student-led learning, teachers will continue to have a vital role in a learner-centered educational system. Teachers will increasingly be tasked with balancing the essential requirements to cultivate community through common experiences, while also generating and implementing customized learning cycles that meet the unique needs of every learner. In short, while institutions will be determining the "what" by identifying the academic standards, key assessments, social-emotional learning frameworks, and providing curricular resources, the system must also support teachers and provide the flexible conditions that will enable them to determine the "how" of students' learning experiences so that they meet the needs of learners in their classrooms.

## What Is the Impact?

Learner-centered education is effective, as the data shows. The LEAP Innovations website, for example, includes numerous references to research that documents the efficacy of this approach. At Altitude Learning, we recently published a document entitled "Evidence of Impact," which includes references to our roots as AltSchool, where we operated a network of K–8 lab schools in San Francisco and New York.[3] In 2018, at the schools that AltSchool operated, the mean growth on the widely used Measure of Academic Progress (MAP) test was 134 percent across all subjects (100 percent is the national average), with strong results on student surveys related to growth mindset, the learner's belief that they can become smarter.

During my tenure as superintendent (2012–2017), the approach we implemented in Vista Unified resulted in reductions in chronic absenteeism, fewer discipline incidents, higher levels of college and career readiness, dramatic increases in learners opting into higher levels of challenge in Advanced Placement and International Baccalaureate courses, and improved graduation rates. Perceptions of our schools, reported by students, classified staff, teachers, administrators, and parents, improved, as indicated by annual survey feedback.

In addition, *Education Week* has run several articles on the evidence of positive impacts in Vista Unified, including titles such as "Measuring the Impact of Personal Learning" and "Numbers to Watch." This accumulation of evidence, coupled with the commonalities across multiple learner-centered models, suggests that we are getting better at identifying and implementing strategies that work. I believe that one of the reasons there is strong alignment across learner-centered models is because these practices work to engage and empower learners, while acknowledging their jagged profiles.

---

[3]https://cdn2.hubspot.net/hubfs/302069/Downloadable%20Marketing%20PDFs/Evidence%20of%20Impact%2010.05.19-1.pdf.

> **Progress on Goals**
>
> **Graduation Rate improved** from 81.1% to 84.8% (2013-2015)
>
> **A-G Completion Rate improved** from 29.4% to 43% (2013-2016)
>
> **AP / IB Participation improved** from 1754 students to 2430 (2013-2016)
>
> **Suspension Rate reduced** from 6% to 2.9% (2012-2015)
>
> **Expulsion Rate reduced** from 0.23% to 0.05% (2012-2015)
>
> **Chronic Absenteeism Rate reduced** from 12.09% to 9.67% (2013-2016)

Data from Vista Unified School District

## Models of Learning

At Vista, when it became clear that we needed a collaborative process to define our model of learning, our team reviewed as many examples as we could find to inspire and inform our thinking. Back in 2013, there were very few models of "personal learning" that we could find. Even so, there were some initial models from agencies like the Gates Foundation and the US Department of Education.

One example came from the Students at the Center Hub, which is funded by the Nellie Mae Education Foundation. While there are some variations, their model similarly prioritizes anytime, anywhere learning and competency-based learning, along with student ownership and personalization.

LEAP Innovations, a national organization based in Chicago that focuses on innovation to transform education, has also developed a framework that includes the following components:

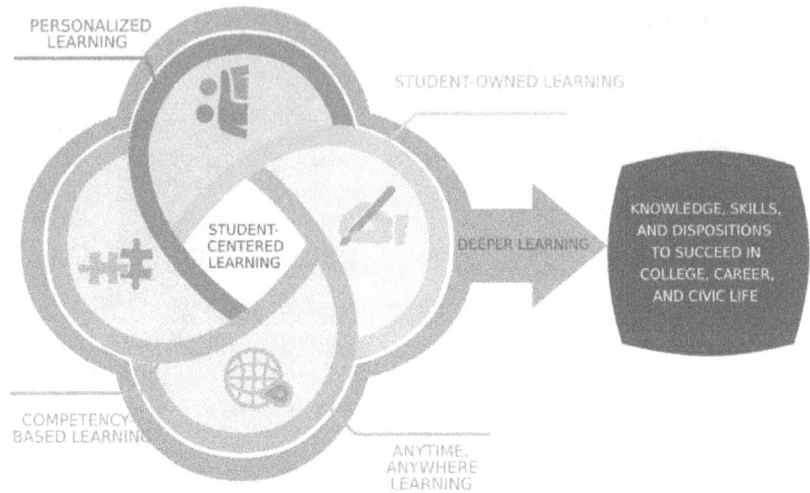

Source: Jobs for the Future (2013). "The Students at the Center Framework." The Students at the Center Hub: https://studentsatthecenterhub.org/interactive-framework/

- Learner-Focused: Students consider their backgrounds, passions, personalities, and needs to experience learning that is relevant and inclusive.
- Learner-Led: Students help shape their individual learning paths and monitor their own progress.
- Learner-Demonstrated: Students progress based on competency, no longer stifled by classrooms that rush them or ask them to wait.
- Learner-Connected: Students supplement classroom learning with real-world experiences, enabling them to thrive in a relationship-driven world.

In the LEAP Innovations model, we again see an emphasis on student self-awareness, learning pathways, competency-based progressions, and real-world experiences.

A more expansive model that reflects many of these same concepts is presented by my Altitude Learning colleague Dr. Katie Martin in

## 10 Characteristics of Learner-Centered Experiences

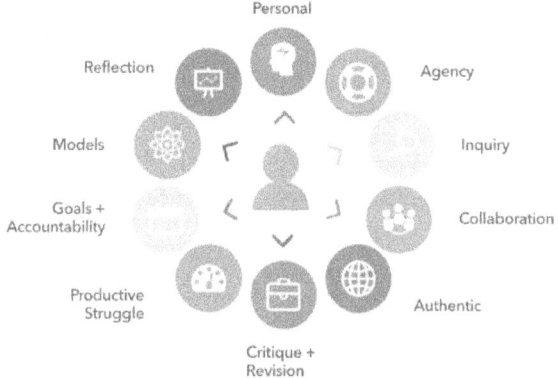

*Learner-Centered Innovation,* Katie Martin, 2018

her 2018 book, *Learner-Centered Innovation*. In addition to agency, collaboration, and authenticity, she adds critical elements such as productive struggle and accountability, which are important components in meaningful learning. I also appreciate the emphasis on reflection in her model, which is implied in other frameworks. Reflection is absolutely essential to promote transfer of learning and metacognition.

One of my favorite frameworks comes from Education Reimagined, a nonprofit that convened a diverse cross-sector group of leaders to develop *A Transformational Vision for Education in the US*. Grounded in the learner-centered paradigm where "learners are active participants in their learning as they gradually become owners of it, and learning itself is seen as an engaging and exciting process," this framework is built on the principles of learner-centered education articulated on their website:

> Learner-centered education is about an entirely new way of seeing, thinking about, and acting on education. It focuses on three key aspects about the learner. First, **each learner is seen as being unique in meaningful ways.** They have unique backgrounds, circumstances, and starting points with unique

strengths, challenges, interests, and aspirations. All of these unique attributes call for unique responses from their learning system. Second, **each learner is seen as having unbounded potential**—potential that will unfold at its own pace and in its own way. Every single learner is a wonder to behold. And, finally, **each learner is seen as having an innate desire to learn. The job of the education system is to unleash that desire.**

The outcome of their visioning process was to define a five-part learning model, which includes competency-based; personalized, relevant, and contextualized; learner agency; socially embedded; and open-walled elements.

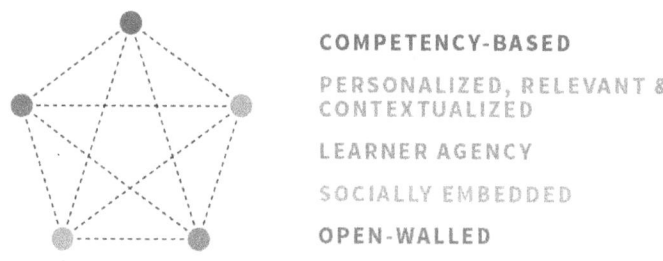

COMPETENCY-BASED

PERSONALIZED, RELEVANT & CONTEXTUALIZED

LEARNER AGENCY

SOCIALLY EMBEDDED

OPEN-WALLED

The Five Elements: A North Star for Learner-Centered Education, Education Reimagined, 2015

## The Vista Star

We called our model the Vista Personal Learning Star. Though it bore similarities to all of the previously discussed models, it was created to fit the particular challenges and goals of our district. It's striking that the Students at the Center framework, LEAP Innovations, and the Learner-Centered Innovation framework all have some individual variations but contain similarities that are beyond coincidental. The emerging consensus in these models indicates an increasing understanding of the critical components of postindustrial education.

The Vista Star contained five points that named areas we thought were crucial to consider: the student profile; technology

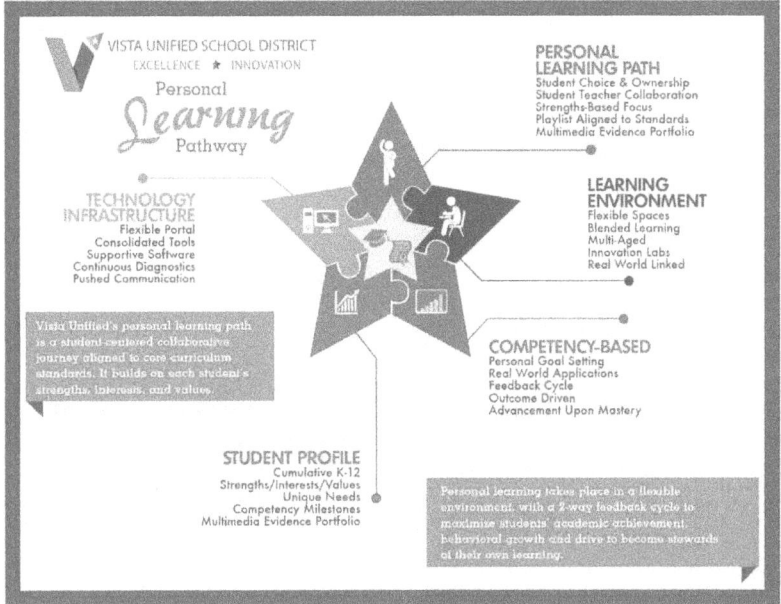

Vista Unified School District Personal Learning Star

infrastructure, personal learning pathways, the learning environment, and competency-based assessment.

The student profile at the base of the star was foundational. In our view, learners would only see the relevance in their learning if and when they get to know themselves as learners. We felt that this profile should also be strengths-based and that it should reference multiple sources of evidence to inform a holistic view of the learner.

Moving clockwise, we felt that it was important to include technology as a component of personal learning. Significantly, technology is an element of the model, but it is not the entirety of the model. Learning is fundamentally social, and it is important to remember that the human dimensions of the learning process should be in the foreground, with technology in the background. For us, we felt that technology could be very helpful in providing continuous diagnostic information about how students are learning, paired with updates pushed to teachers in real time.

| MODEL COMPONENT | CURRENT PARADIGM | LEARNER-CENTERED PARADIGM |
|---|---|---|
| Organization of learners | Organized in age cohorts | Learners learn individually and in diverse and shifting groups consistent with their developmental, social, and competency needs |
| Curricula | Standardized linear curricula divided into subjects | Relevant, contextualized curricula organized by competency |
| Learner goals / Progress indicators | Required credit hours and seat time | Development of competency in agreed domains of knowledge, skills, and dispositions in timeframes appropriate to each learner |
| Role of learners | Passive vessel to be filled | Active co-creators of their learning and development |
| Role of adults | Individual teachers expected to serve as content deliverers, curriculum developers, data assessors | Network of qualified adults facilitating learning and development |

| | | |
|---|---|---|
| Technology | One-to-many communication tools (e.g. books, white boards, projectors) | One-to-one, one-to-many, many-to-many communication, networking, diagnostic, and content delivery tools |
| Assessment | Primarily "of" learning | Intentional assessment "for, as, and of" learning |
| Resource Allocation | Place- and formula-based funding uncorrelated with individual children's needs | Financial resources applied and integrated to support the whole child |
| Location | Localized in a school building | Learning occurs at many times, in many places, and through many formats; a physical space is established for learners and adults to gather, socialize, and learn |
| Meeting learner's needs | Differentiation of the standard model to meet learners' needs | Personalization for each and every learner |

Source: *Education Reimagined, A Transformational Vision for Education in the US*, 2015: https://education-reimagined.org/wp-content/uploads/2019/01/Vision_Website.pdf.

At the top of the star we have the personal learning path, which is where the element of student choice helps the learner to engage in self-directed and self-driven learning. We also felt it was important to convey that learning would be connected to standards and would be done in a collaborative fashion.

Next we recognized that we would need flexible learning environments, including real-world connections, in order to shift to personal learning for all. Rows of desks facing a teacher are too rigid and inflexible to create the conditions for learners to engage in authentic, relevant, and personal interactions.

Rounding out our star is competency-based learning, where learners set their own goals and then advance upon mastering content, which is intended to allow students to move at their own rates. Connecting to our mission statement, we also felt it was critical to emphasize real-world applications as part of this competency-based approach.

The Vista Star's five-part model helped us to have a framework that would allow us to shift our practices in ways that were fundamentally designed to ensure relevance for all learners.

## Synthesis

There is clear alignment between four points of the Vista Star with elements from Education Reimagined's framework. The one point of divergence is that the Vista model included technology, and Education Reimagined includes socially embedded learning.

I am now of the opinion that Education Reimagined's framework is a better model for several reasons. The elevation of the social process of learning is helpful in rebutting misperceptions about whether learner-centered practices result in what is effectively an independent study experience for all. I have also come to better understand that technology should be in the background for each of these elements, serving to support and enhance competency-based approaches, personalization, the cultivation of learner agency, socially embedded learning, and open-walled experiences. In short, if I could go back in time and modify the Vista Star, I would swap out technology and add socially embedded learning.

Impressively, Education Reimagined's vision document also clarifies that "these five elements are not meant to serve as a blueprint for a rigid model to be implemented everywhere. Instead, they serve as a 'North Star' to guide innovation. They do not create a single roadmap that can be followed the same way in every learning community." This approach is consistent with what we learned in Vista as we implemented our model. It is exceptionally helpful to have a guiding framework, and as we learned from feedback, not so helpful to have a centrally imposed prescription for how to transform pedagogy and practice.

Another component to the Education Reimagined vision document is an acknowledgement that there are components of education that can support or impede the implementation of learner-centric instructional models. It is critical for leaders to understand that these model components must be re-examined and adjusted locally to achieve the transformational potential of learner-centered education.

## Systemic Transformation

We are at an exciting moment in time where there is emerging consensus on the key elements of a learner-centric model of education. While the terms vary in different models, concepts such as a strong sense of self, pathways, flexible learning environments, and competency-based and socially embedded learning are quickly becoming the critical underpinnings of a postindustrial education. Evidence that this empowering approach results in measurable improvements is accumulating across the United States: in Chicago (LEAP Innovation), San Francisco and New York (AltSchool), and in suburbs like Vista.

> **Technology and Agency**
>
> It is also important to be thoughtful about the role of technology in a learner-centered educational system, while keeping people in the foreground and technology in the background. This intentional ordering is imperative because we are social creatures, and powerful learning is predominantly a social experience. Humans are making decisions at the institutional and teacher levels with the goal of creating the conditions needed for learners to make their own decisions to drive their learning. At each of these levels, institutions, teachers, and learners can benefit from technology that creates efficiencies and informs decision-making by providing access to evidence that promotes deeper understanding, more targeted planning, deeper engagement, and profound assessments. It should be noted that decision-makers for institutions are generally designed to represent their community. In other words, people make decisions for institutions. Although technology is powerful, it is necessary to examine the role it plays and where it can be most impactful in the learning experience.
>
> Technology falls into one of the buckets of "agency"—the ownership of different parts of the educational system and learning experiences:

If these examples provide us with an accessible and inspiring framework for what the future holds, the challenge in leadership is to create the conditions to make it happen. In the next chapters, we'll see that although systematic transformation is not easy, it is possible.

## Resources

- https://education-reimagined.org/collections/what-is-learner-centered-education/
- Altitude Learning blog series, by Colleen Broderick

| Where Is the Agency? | |
| --- | --- |
| Institution | "What" <br> Academic standards <br> Social-emotional learning frameworks <br> Key assessments <br> Dynamic curriculum |
| Teacher | "How" <br> Learning designers <br> Relationships <br> Classroom culture |
| Learner | Understanding <br> Planning <br> Engaging <br> Assessing <br> Collaborating <br> Revising |
| Technology | Informing decisions made by people at institutional, teacher, and learner levels <br> Improving efficiency <br> Making learning visible <br> Managing/tracking progress |

- "Why Personalized Learning?" from LEAP Innovations
- Learner-Centered Innovation blog, by Dr. Katie Martin

## KEY QUESTIONS:

- How do the learning models presented align with your current model? What would you revise or add to your learning model?

- How might we better support the shift from teacher-led to student-driven learning?
- How might we reimagine classrooms, schools, and districts to embrace multiple pathways and self-paced learning where students are in "driving" mode?
- How are we ensuring that technology is supporting efficiencies and informing decisions made by people such as school leaders, educators, and learners?

Please use the hashtag #LCLeadership and share your responses on social media.

# 2

# A FRAMEWORK FOR THE FUTURE

To lead, there must be a call to a desired future. This future orientation can be operationalized by what I call a "Framework for the Future," which is larger in scope than the "blueprint" I employed at Vista. This framework includes a shared vision, mission, values, goals, roles and responsibilities, and a strategic plan (or blueprint). We sometimes confuse these terms, so allow me to provide the following concise definitions:

- Vision: where we are going
- Mission: why we exist
- Values: how we will behave on the journey
- Goals: measurable outcomes that help us to know if we are making progress
- Roles and responsibilities: who is accountable for the progress we make
- Strategic plan: a set of strategies, actions, and resource allocations that will help us to make progress

Sometimes circumstances mean a leader must create and share their own Framework for the Future, but the most desirable approach is to co-construct one in a way that helps a community have collective ownership. This inclusive model is slower at the beginning, yet it tends to be far more effective over time than a more traditional "tell 'em and sell 'em" approach.

It is also important to be comprehensive and ensure that there are no gaps in the Framework for the Future. Consider, for example, the Knoster Model (below), which illustrates what happens when key elements are missing. Many of us have had such experiences—false starts, frustration, resistance, anxiety, and confusion. By ensuring clarity up front for essential areas like vision, mission, values, goals, roles and responsibilities, and strategic plans, we find that we can achieve what we want: success!

**Knoster Model**

| Vision | Skills | Incentives | Resources | Action Plan | = | Success |
|--------|--------|------------|-----------|-------------|---|---------|
| Vision | Skills | Incentives | Resources |             | = | False Starts |
| Vision | Skills | Incentives |           | Action Plan | = | Frustration |
| Vision | Skills |            | Resources | Action Plan | = | Resistance |
| Vision |        | Incentives | Resources | Action Plan | = | Anxiety |
|        | Skills | Incentives | Resources | Action Plan | = | Confusion |

In Vista, the process we used to develop the components for our Framework for the Future was equally critical. In my experience as a school leader, people own what they create. So, we designed and implemented an interactive and inclusive approach.

Once we got the green light from the school board to proceed with the development of the Framework for the Future, my first action was to use a "social host model" to find out who wanted to help with the initial design. In the social host model, the leader begins with an open invitation to a wide group, then engages those who choose to attend in a process to explore possibilities for the future. I began with our management team, which included around one hundred administrators. I sent an open invitation asking if they would like to come and join a creative session on our Framework for the Future. About twenty of our administrators participated in that first meeting, with roles ranging from assistant superintendents to assistant principals.

We started by sharing definitions of the key terms (such as *vision* and *mission*) and examples of vision documents, mission statements, values, and measurable goals from other settings. We discussed the need for a balance between urgency and high levels of participation from the community. I told the group that I wanted to create a single sentence that represented our vision, mission, and values. I wanted something that could be easily memorized and would be more likely to serve as a meaningful reference during the work ahead. I also invited the group to consider whether we should stage the process into different sections. We then broke into small groups to brainstorm plans.

The collective wisdom of the team far surpassed what any individual would have generated in isolation. We decided to combine vision, mission, and values into a consolidated push that would take about four months to complete. We would launch the process with a town hall community meeting. There, several leaders would present the rationale for why it was important for us to be clear on what we wanted for the future. From there, attendees would rotate through a "World Café" model, where facilitators at different tables would ask questions related to the vision, mission, and values. For example, a vision question would be something like: "How do you want Vista Unified School District to be described in the year 2030?" A mission question might be: "What is the purpose of public education?" A values question might be: "How should we make difficult decisions?"

We scheduled the town hall meeting for mid-September, after the students were back in school. We invited community leaders such as the mayor and the city manager, the police chief and fire captain, the CEO of the Chamber of Commerce, leaders from the local community college and California State University, early education providers, the Parent Teacher Association, our District English Learner Advisory Committee, the Vista Teachers Association, and the California School Employees Association. We also invited the district's legal team to participate. Most importantly, we invited students.

This meeting was also designed to be interactive. As a result, participants from a variety of perspectives and backgrounds provided tons of input and generated incredible ideas. One of the attendees, a veteran teacher who had seen many of the missteps that the Knoster table illustrates, said he felt hopeful for the future for the first time in many years.

It was important not to lose the momentum from that launch and to show the attendees that their input was leading to significant next steps. So, our volunteer team of administrators came back together (and actually grew a bit as word of the successful launch started to spread) and began to synthesize the input we received into draft vision, mission, and values statements. In our attempt to be comprehensive, the first few drafts were voluminous, with one of the early versions of the vision statement spanning two pages of dense text!

At this point, we engaged the community through online surveys, social media posts, and updates through our school board meetings. We posted revisions to solicit feedback, and we went back to small groups to continue to refine and consolidate important themes. Within about two months, we distilled the town hall input and thousands of survey comments into the following declarations:

> Vista Unified School District will be the model of educational excellence and innovation.

A FRAMEWORK FOR THE FUTURE

Community input, Vista Unified School District Town Hall Meeting, 2012

The purpose of the Vista Unified School District is to inspire every student to persevere as a critical thinker who collaborates to solve real-world problems.

Our values will be respect, trust, and collaboration. *Respect* means treating all with dignity. *Trust* means having confidence that every decision is made in the best interests of all students. *Collaboration* is working in collective partnership with clear two-way dialogue that builds relationships among home, school, and the community.

When I share these statements with other school leaders, I emphasize that the point here is not to say that every school or district should have this vision, mission, and values. Nor would every community follow the same process step-by-step. My intent is to make explicit that every learning community should be very clear about

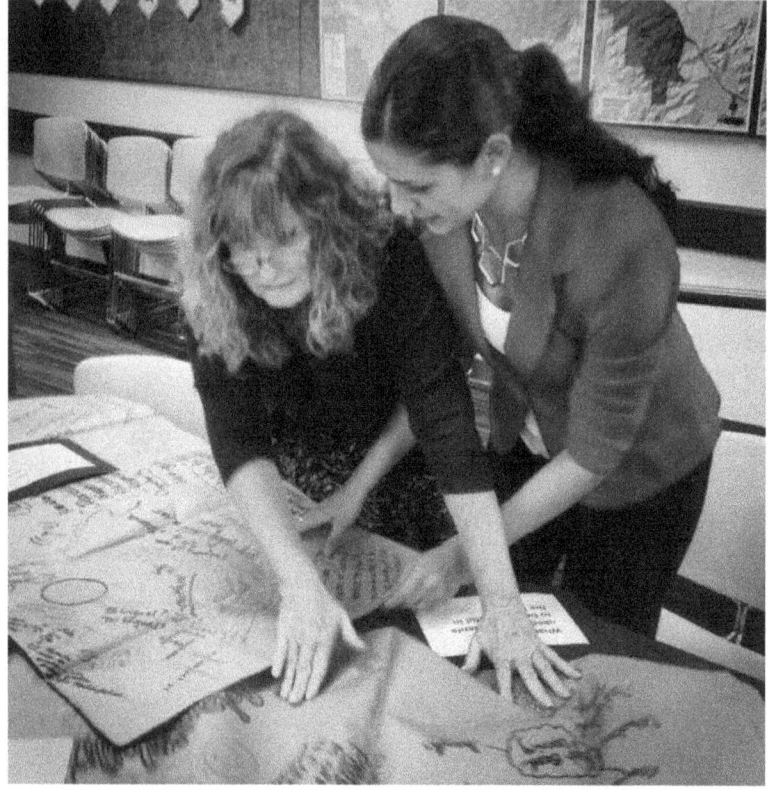

Synthesizing community input, Vista Unified School District, 2012

their own vision, mission, and values and should create an interactive, fluid approach to soliciting and refining input. For our school district with about twenty-five thousand students, the entire journey from conception to board approval took less than six months. It set the stage for the next five years in ways that I could not have imagined at that time.

## Goals

At this point, I was energized by the aspirational language of these foundational elements of the Framework of the Future. But I am also pragmatic enough to know that simply stating you want to be "the model of educational excellence and innovation" won't make it happen. It would take a long time to achieve that lofty ambition.

Along the way, we needed indicators of progress that would enable us to know if we were on or off track. Next came the goal-setting stage. This took about three months from initial draft recommendations until board approval. In this case, I felt it was essential that the school board owned the goals. As elected representatives of the community, it was their job to hold us accountable for ongoing improvements. Therefore, I had less broad input on this phase of the process and more extensive engagement with the board, including a special working session devoted exclusively to the development and refinement of the goals.

My interest was to ensure that the goals were measurable and time-bound. More importantly, I wanted to ensure that the goals aligned with our vision, mission, and values. In addition, I wanted us to have only a few well-defined goals so that we could be focused in our efforts moving forward.

Initially, we landed at a place where we had strong alignment, but perhaps too many goals; this was a good early lesson in the process. Even with an aligned five-member board, each individual had particular interests and wanted to see those expressed as a specific goal. The combined impact of our common goals plus roughly five individually driven goals resulted in a list that was too long to provide the clarity we needed. In addition, the initial draft did not include any prioritization, which made it difficult to know how to focus time and resources to support the abundance of outcomes that had been identified. To reconcile this tension, we made adjustments, such as placing the goals into priority categories. That way, we could emphasize the most critical goals in our plans and through the reporting cycles to the board.

In addition to measures of student learning, we also included goals that related to our Framework for the Future. We ensured that we measured levels of respect, trust, and collaboration through surveys of students, families, and staff to show critical alignment with our values. We also measured "real-world problem solving" (through participation in service-learning projects, career technical education, and applied science and social studies courses), which was such an important part of our mission. In terms of our vision, we felt that attracting and retaining students was a good measure of our reputation for excellence and innovation. In cases where measurements did not exist, we developed metrics that made sense and used those as baselines to gauge progress. Having goals is one thing; however, actually using them to drive ongoing improvement is another.

Our school board took the lead and established a cadence where every meeting would begin with an update on the progress related to one or two of our goals. The highest-priority goals were reviewed with greater frequency and intensity. The board meeting practice of regular progress reviews related to goals cascaded through our leadership meetings, and soon we saw school site plans aligning with the district metrics.

Importantly, the presence and guiding force of the goals emphasized student learning with outcomes related to areas like English language arts, mathematics, science, technology, art, service learning, and career technical education. The goals further articulated an expectation that students would take more difficult classes such as Advanced Placement and International Baccalaureate courses. They expanded the definition and metrics of success, emphasizing the importance of attendance, positive behavior, and graduating more students who were ready for college and career and life. For everything that came next—including our ambitious innovation efforts—the success or failure of our initiatives was grounded by the goals that always brought us back to our learners.

Vista Unified School District
Goals Proposal – February 2016

| Priority | Goal | | Metric | State Priority | 2012-13 Actual | 2013-14 Actual | 2014-15 Actual | 2015-16 Goal | 2016-17 Goal | 2017-18 Goal |
|---|---|---|---|---|---|---|---|---|---|---|
| Highest Priority | 1 | 1a | Reading/Writing Proficiency Rate | 4 | 54.1% (CST) | N/A | 41% (SBAC) | 45% | 49% | 53% |
| | | 1b | Reclassification Percentage of EL Students at 5 years | 4 | 21% | 25% | 27% | 30% | 33% | 36% |
| | 2 | 2a | Mathematics Proficiency Rate | 4 | 57.5% (CST) | N/A | 29% (SBAC) | 32% | 35% | 38% |
| | 3 | 3a | Graduation Rate | 5 | 81.1% | 82.6% | NA* | 86% | 88% | 90% |
| | | 3b | A-G Completion Rate | 4 | 29.4% | 29.9% | NA* | 33% | 36% | 39% |
| | | 3c | High School Students Enrolled in One or More AP/IB Courses | 4 | 1,754 | 1,981 | 2,028 | 2,430** | 2,550 | 2,700 |
| | | 3d | Advanced Placement Passing Rate | 4 | 48.7% | 48.2% | 48.8% | 51%** | 54% | 57% |
| | 4 | 4a | Service Learning Participation | 8 | NA | NA | 250 | 850** | 1,200 | 1,600 |
| | | 4b | CTE Participation | 7 | NA | NA | NA | NA | TBD | TBD |
| | | 4c | Civic Engagement | 8 | NA | NA | NA | NA | TBD | TBD |
| High Priority | 5 | 5a | Science Participation | 7 | NA | NA | 5,019 | 5,425** | 5,600 | 5,700 |
| | | 5b | Technology Participation | 7 | NA | NA | 1,551 | 1,676** | 1,750 | 1,800 |
| | | 5c | Engineering Participation | 7 | NA | NA | 284 | 350** | 375 | 400 |
| | | 5d | Visual and Performing Arts Participation | 7 | NA | NA | 2,597 | 2,562** | 2,600 | 2,650 |
| | 6 | 6a | Attendance Rate | 5 | 95.90% | 96.19% | 95.84% | 96.35% | 97.0% | 97.5% |
| | | 6b | Chronic Absenteeism | 5 | 12.09% | 11.93% | 12.93% | 12.67%*** | <10% | <9% |
| | | 6c | Suspension/Expulsion Rate | 6 | 5.7% / 0.11% | 3.9% / 0.07% | 2.9% / 0.05% | <2% / <0.1% | <2% / <0.1% | <2% / <0.1% |
| | | 6d | Drop-out Rate | 5 | 9.0% | 9.5% | NA* | <8.6% | <8.1% | <7.5% |
| | 7 | 7a | Survey Results | 6 | TBD | TBD | TBD | TBD | TBD | TBD |
| | 8 | 8a | Williams Compliance Results | 1 | Compliant | Compliant | Compliant | Compliant | Compliant | Compliant |
| | 9 | 9a | Net gain/loss in student population through interdistrict transfer process | 5 | +126 | +106 | +300 | +236*** | +270 | +300 |
| | | 9b | Students who reside within VUSD who select charter schools | 5 | NA | NA | NA | NA | TBD | TBD |

*Official rates to be released in late-April 2016. **Actual figure, not a goal; ***Rate/figure as of Feb. 5, 2016

Goals, Vista Unified School District, 2016

## Roles and Responsibilities

The next phase was to determine roles and responsibilities. In other words, who would be accountable for our making progress relative to the goals that aligned with our vision, mission, and values? This was a challenging phase of the Framework for the Future because it began to become evident that change would be required for us to achieve our aspirations. We also realized that we needed a culture of accountability to ensure that we progressed as fast as possible for the benefit of our students.

The superintendent is the lone hire from the school board, so ultimately, I was the person who was accountable for success. As a result, while I did a few brainstorming sessions with our leadership team during this phase, it was chiefly my own project. I needed a structure that made sense to me and that would also give us the best chance of meaningful improvement. Here, I must confess that I am energized by futuristic thinking, and therefore I buried myself in learning about new-age organizational models such as holacracies, microcommunities, and other concepts, like self-managed teams. While some of those approaches held intellectual appeal, I was not convinced at that stage that we would be able to navigate a massive reorganizational process. I was even less convinced that it would be the type of initiative that would have a swift and positive impact on our learners.

I proposed to the board a relatively modest realignment of our central office roles and responsibilities. We would expand from the traditional three-department model that typifies most school districts, with a curriculum and instruction department, human resources department, and business department, to a four-department team that would align with our vision, mission, and values. More specifically, we would have one department focused on educational excellence, another on innovation, another on human relations, and the fourth on business services. The adjustments in Business Services were minor. The reframing away from "human resources" to "human relations" was mostly symbolic, intended to convey that our people are not resources, and instead we should focus on the importance of the relationships that reflect our values of respect, trust, and collaboration. However, the creation of an innovation department was a very new concept for our district, and for many others that I was connected with at that time.

It may be helpful here to acknowledge that not all who read this text will be in a superintendent role. At every level of an org chart, individuals are part of teams and they are embedded in existing formal structures that were designed and implemented by people. Regardless of your role in an organization, you can influence the official roles and responsibilities through actions and advocacy. Teachers, for example, can be mindful about the roles and responsibilities of learners in a classroom. Site-level administrators can have a similar view with respect to school-level structures. Directors and assistant superintendents have teams that can be reimagined and restructured.

The inspiration to create the Innovation Department was grounded in my many experiences of trying to promote innovative practices, while feeling as if most of my time was being spent dealing with urgent and immediate tasks with nonnegotiable requirements. One of my most memorable experiences was when I was a curriculum director and had returned from an inspiring professional learning experience. I came back eager and excited to try new approaches that held great potential for improvement. Instead, I found myself spending the next few days completing compliance tasks for categorical funds and feeling that these efforts were very disconnected from anything that would have a direct impact on learning.

It's nearly impossible to function in both strategic and execution mode simultaneously on a long-term basis. There are many resources on how to create a culture of innovation, and many of them recognize that the day-to-day requirements of most jobs impede the creative thinking that is necessary to fuel meaningful innovation. Outside of schools, it is fairly common practice to embrace a "skunk works" mentality where small teams are relieved of their regular duties, placed far away from the main office, and asked to engage in a complex challenge with minimal constraints and guidance. This is precisely the intent that I had in mind with the creation of our Innovation Department.

In the early stages, the department was one person (remember: start small but get started!). There was literally no space for that person at the district office, so he was placed at a remote location. While this created some challenges with coordination, the benefits of that separation outweighed those disadvantages. It quickly became obvious that placing a high-performing leader in this position was going to stretch all of us (including him) to reconsider how we would function, in a way that promoted transformation as well as incremental improvements.

My last note on roles and responsibilities is that language matters. Just as it was important for us to shift from "human resources" to "human relations," it was also important to call our instructional team the "Department of Educational Excellence." I did not want to reinforce the notion that simply by providing a curricular program and an instructional model, the work of that department was complete. If we wanted to achieve educational excellence, we would need to be oriented to learner outcomes. In order to achieve excellence, those outcomes would need to exceed expectations.

Finally, in my proposal for roles and responsibilities, we organized the school principals into teams. This was purposefully done to align with our value of collaboration. It also conveyed a message that we would need to think differently about how site leaders interacted with one another if we were to achieve our aspirations to be the model of educational excellence and innovation.

I should also make it clear that this articulation of roles and responsibilities seems very undeveloped in our complex educational settings. While there are obviously many influences on the experience and outcomes for any learner, my intent was to minimize

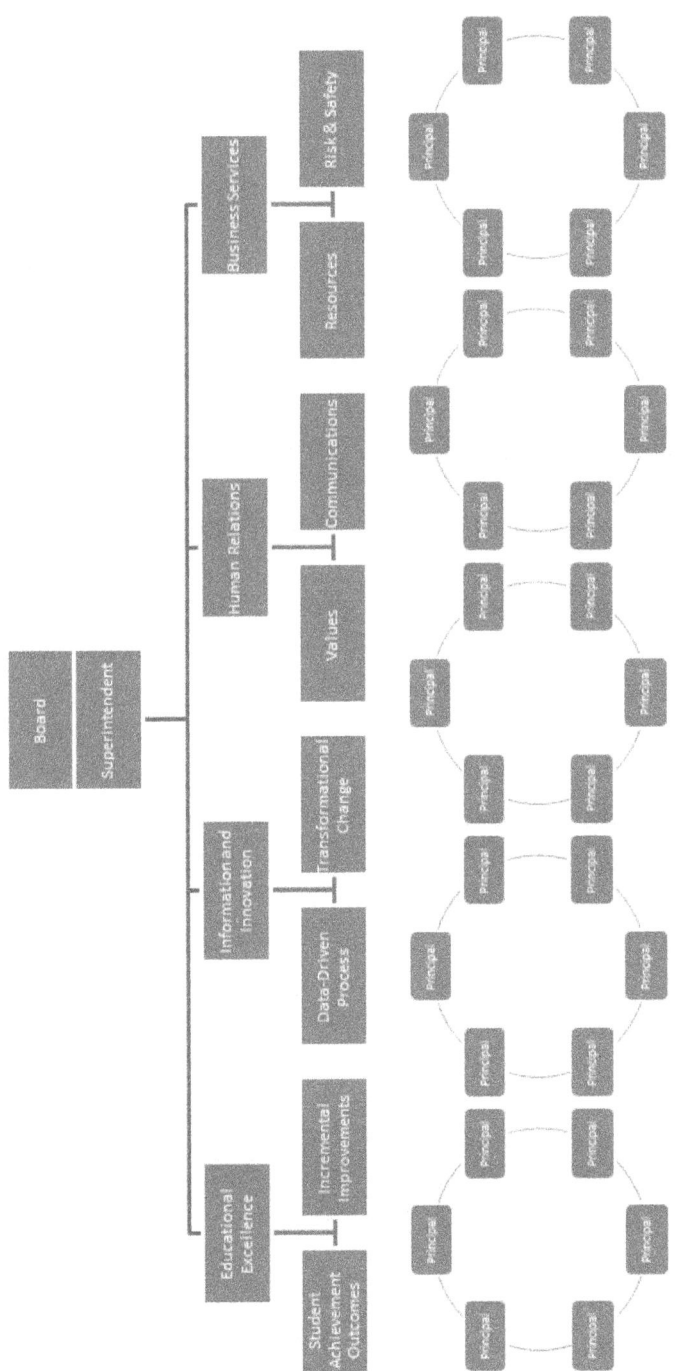

Roles and Responsibilities, Vista Unified School District, 2013

confusion about how we would create structures that promoted internal accountability. Some of this may have been self-protective—I knew that I was the one person that the board would hold accountable if we fell short of achieving our aspirations. But it is also again reflected in my own experience in various leadership roles in education. We sometimes fell victim to two unproductive extremes. In the first, "everyone" was accountable for particular outcomes, which meant that nobody was truly accountable. In the second, the actual accountability was so misaligned from the stated roles that it was fundamentally counterproductive.

I strongly believe that our best performance comes from making performance quality visible, and that requires clear expectations and systems to ensure ongoing productivity and improvement. Grounded in our goals for redefining the experience for all learners, I wanted to have clear targets and measures to create the conditions that would foster individual accountability as we moved forward to achieve our collective goals. It is also important to emphasize here that our goals that aligned with our vision, mission, and values could then be assigned to these departments to create very clear ownership and accountability.

In summary, I want to reiterate that the ways in which other leaders should organize their roles and responsibilities should not mirror the exact structures we created in Vista. The roles and responsibilities in any setting should align with the vision, mission, values, and goals in that particular context. By cascading from vision, mission, and values to goals that can be used to measure progress, roles can be clarified and individuals can be accountable for their performance on those goals. These leadership imperatives are essential to create the conditions for success.

## Blueprint

A clear sense of our destination (vision), our purpose (mission), how we want to behave (values), how to measure progress (goals), and who is responsible for that progress (roles and responsibilities)—these are all foundational elements that guide the development of a strategic plan. Unfortunately, even those elements are not sufficient to move teams, organizations, and communities through complex change. Having a plan to drive collective action is a necessary, critical component that can create focus and clarity, and catalyze ongoing learning about the connections between activities and outcomes.

I have previously described the origins and intent of our blueprint process. After ensuring that there was support from the school board to proceed, we made a list of those groups that would be affected by the blueprint. This initially included community leaders, parents, school leadership, teachers, staff, and students. We then expanded out. For some groups, like parents, there were existing networks, such as the PTA, the District Parent Advisory Committee, and the District English Learner Advisory Committee, that could be engaged and activated to assist with the development process. At this stage, I admit that while we broadened the net to include these groups, I anticipated that we would hear similar messages to those we had already been receiving through these traditional channels. To my surprise, their input turned out to be invaluable and pushed us to think in new and meaningful ways. This was a humbling lesson for me, and I encourage all leaders to push themselves to widen the circle to seek additional perspective when developing plans.

Dr. Matt Doyle, who was the innovation lead, facilitated the process of implementing our blueprint for change. He and I spent some time doing a "roadshow" in our schools and in the community to share the first draft of the blueprint. That generated some frank feedback, which led us to reconsider how to begin to create momentum.

We learned that our initial, text-heavy drafts were generally inaccessible and unintelligible. As indicated earlier, the student forums proved to be a profoundly impactful experience and one that motivated an ambitious call to action.

We found it necessary to create and use visuals, such as the "House of Learning," (see page 69) to tell the story of what we planned to do in pursuit of our vision. Knowing that we were competing to keep the attention of our community, we also produced brief videos (about three minutes each) to explain each of the strategies, using interviews and examples.

At one point, a board member asked how they would be apprised of progress as we implemented the plan. This led us to schedule monthly updates at each board meeting to review the process, implementation progress, and any outcome data that we were associating with our efforts. This routine of public, open updates helped us to create a culture of accountability and to ensure that we maintained a sustained focus on doing what we had said we would do.

In addition to the board updates, we posted everything related to the blueprint on the Vista Unified School District website. Meeting notes, agendas, timelines, draft plans—everything was made transparent in the hopes that it would promote openness and inclusion.

I also encouraged Dr. Doyle to find a way to organize the plan digitally so that we could have real-time access to track implementation. He worked with a small firm that created custom software that we could use to document and monitor the plan. Dr. Doyle also worked with strategic planning consultants who helped us to organize the plan into strategies, action plans, action steps, and associated finances. Each strategy, action plan, and action step had a clear owner who aligned with our roles and responsibilities. The blueprint truly became the plan of action for our team, creating a common language and consistent structure for ongoing improvements.

Importantly, the blueprint also became a filtering mechanism for new initiatives. If it wasn't in the plan, we took the ideas and ran through a process to consider including them in the next revision of the blueprint. The plan was organized into a three-year cycle, with the intent to update annually. After about six months, we realized that the plan was actually too restrictive, so we modified it to provide some flexibility on the details (particularly in terms of reallocating resources when our initial estimates were incorrect) while remaining rigid on the overall constructs.

We created a "Blueprint Construction Network" to assist in prioritizing the new ideas, determining which of the existing plans required updates, and to recommend changes to each of the annual updates to the blueprint. Following the spirit of the initial consultations, we made sure that we had community representatives, students, parents, teachers, classified staff members, and school leaders participating and providing input for these important decisions. I should note that we maintained a structure where this input was advisory to me, and I would then make a recommendation to the school board for official approval. This process worked fairly efficiently. The only challenges we experienced were when we became lax in reminding the group about their advisory nature and the overall process.

Around this time, the California accountability model was shifting to a "local control" approach that included a "Local Control Accountability Plan" (LCAP), which had many of the same general components as our blueprint. Working with our software provider, Dr. Doyle found a way to export our plan into the required LCAP template, integrating our existing process into the new accountability requirements in an incredibly efficient manner.

Just as individuals with diverse job titles can influence roles and responsibilities, plans also exist at multiple levels of an organization. Teachers have plans for their classrooms and site administrators have plans for their schools. District administrators often have program or service plans. In every case, the fundamentals of an impactful approach are an inclusive development process, transparency at every stage of implementation, and mechanisms to solicit feedback and make adjustments. Finally, connecting and aligning plans with emerging requirements is a way to ensure that there is focus and coherence in a changing context.

Having a plan turns out to be extremely important. I knew that our aspirations were big and that it would take many, many years to achieve our vision. Connecting that vision with our "why" (the mission), our "how" (the values), our goals, and the roles and responsibilities that culminated in a comprehensive, inclusive, and ambitious plan had the effect of connecting our desired future with our present state. It helped us go from dreams to reality. It also helped us to see the path forward. Now that we had a framework for the future, it was time to move.

> For more info on the Vista blueprint: http://www.vistausd.org/blueprint.

## KEY QUESTIONS:

- How might we better listen to our learners?
- How might you improve clarity and consensus on the vision, mission, and values in your context?
- How might you improve alignment between goals, roles and responsibilities, and the vision/mission/values?
- How might you improve use of your strategic plan to drive ongoing improvement?
- How might you strengthen the link between resource allocation and the strategies/actions in your plan?
- How might you share the vision, mission, values, goals, roles/responsibilities, and strategic plan, using multiple channels such as visuals, videos, and analogies?

Please use the hashtag #LCLeadership and share your responses on social media.

# 3

# FROM LEARNER-CENTERED EDUCATION TO LEADERSHIP

At one point in my work at Vista, I had been wrestling with the question of what to do about an underperforming middle school that we were converting into a magnet school. Washington Middle School had for many years been in program improvement status. Student enrollment was shrinking every year as families were increasingly opting to send their children to other sites. The facility was aging and in need of attention. On my first visit to the school, I was told that it was a gang-infested area and that I needed to watch for my safety. Many of the staff members appeared to be exhausted and burned out.

The principal of Washington Middle had left for another district during the first week of school and, near the middle of the year, I hired Dr. Eric Chagala, one of the high school assistant principals from within the district, to become the new principal. During his interview for the job, I mentioned that this was a very difficult principalship. It would either be very short and end poorly, or it would be a massive undertaking that would result in significant transformation. This was not an easy job for a first-time principal. Eric's response: "I could have applied to be principal at other schools, and I have not pursued those options. The fact that this is a difficult one is exactly why I want this job." I knew in that moment he was the right person for the challenges ahead.

One of his first priorities was to work with his community to identify a theme for the school. We had already engaged a community group to help us identify magnet pathways to build on our existing programs, and we had settled on STEM, the arts, and International Baccalaureate (IB). I believed that the school needed a strong identity to help generate enthusiasm and excitement as we worked to improve the learning experience. I had expected Eric to come back with something like a computer science focus or to go with a known model like IB.

Instead, Eric had worked with the community and brought forward a proposal for a design-thinking school. This was at the start of 2013. *Design thinking* was a completely new term for me. Eric described it as the intersection of arts and STEM, and a perfect fit into our magnet pathways. Considering that I had not heard of design thinking, I was skeptical that our community would rally around the concept. Picking the wrong focus would likely be the end of this struggling school. The safe choice was to say no. But saying no also didn't feel right.

I'm not sure how much I let on that I was not initially enthusiastic about the design-thinking idea. I hope that I portrayed curiosity and interest in learning more. But my initial instinct and rational response was definitely that this was a bad idea. My intuition was also signaling to me that I should not make a quick decision. I gave myself a bit of time to let the idea incubate before I made the call. It was in those sleepless nights that I decided to say yes and to support the recommendation from Eric and his team.

Fast forward a few years, and the Vista Innovation and Design Academy (or VIDA, which also means "life" in Spanish) was the fastest-improving school in the district. We had gone from a school with declining enrollment to one with wait lists of hundreds of students each year. It was, and continues to be, one of the most frequently visited schools in the region. By every metric, it has been an incredible success and one that was achieved with the same facility and same staff that we had had in the past. The new focus on design thinking, coupled with incredible work by the teachers and staff, catalyzed an unbelievable transformation in the learning experience. And it almost didn't happen because my initial instinct had been to say no and to make a safer choice with less risk.

When I reflect on why this story has such a positive outcome, the context for these interactions matters. At the end of the day, the reason that I supported the proposal from Eric was that I trusted him. I also think that he felt safe enough to bring an unconventional idea forward because he trusted me. My trust in him was rooted in every one of our interactions, including the interview, where I had the distinct impression that he genuinely wanted to make a difference in the lives of kids and that he cared a great deal for the community. I would like to think that he felt comfortable introducing a new concept because he had seen that we shared similar commitments and that I had been open to other new ideas.

Trust matters. Relationships matter. Learner-centered leaders focus on trust and relationships first to set the conditions for transformation.

## What Is Leadership?

Once the conditions for change are in place and the strategic elements of the Framework of the Future are set, it is important to consider how to implement the plans in ways that are likely to achieve the desired improvements. This is where leadership becomes critical. Taking the view that schools and school systems are living systems that are not dependent on a central authority, I should be clear that my view of leadership is completely independent of title or position. Catalysts for change can come from anywhere. We all exert influence on one another, and, in spite of the illusion of control, we are always fundamentally interacting with other individuals who also have agency. As stated by organizational consultants Margaret Wheatley and Myron Kellner-Rogers, "You can never direct a living system, you can only disturb it."

It reminds me of the classic book by leadership guru Ronald Heifetz, *Leadership Without Easy Answers*, which provides strong examples of highly influential leaders who were successful without formal positions or titles. Gandhi and Martin Luther King Jr. are two very notable illustrations that reinforce the incredible influence that arises through building credibility and modeling an ethical approach. In modern times, I think of someone like Malala Yousafzai, who similarly exerts strong influence with absolutely no position of official authority.

## Servant Leadership

If Malala can serve as a strong example of leadership, each of us can be leaders. In my view, her success (and that of many others) is largely due to her service to a broader mission. While she leads, she also serves a cause. In short, leadership is a form of service. I would posit that successful leaders are servant-leaders.

Servant leadership was a concept originally popularized by Robert Greenleaf after he read *Siddhartha*, which led him to insights regarding the influence of "servants" who exerted strong influence and leadership. While some see servant leadership from a status perspective and presume that it functions in service to other people, my view is that servant leadership exists in service to values.

This perspective was informed in large part due to a collaboration between our school district and the Servant Leadership Institute (SLI) in San Diego. We engaged with SLI to provide training for all leaders in the school district (including a series for new hires), to elevate our common understanding of the need for values-based leadership. Given our core values of respect, trust, and collaboration, this inevitably led back to a relational frame.[4]

Servant leadership does not rely on positional authority. It is reliant on the embodiment of values that elevate others. One of my favorite examples of servant leadership as a superintendent was a program that our community ran every other year called "Vista's Big Give." This program was primarily driven by two teachers—Beth Duncan and Kelly McKinney—who organized teams of students from schools throughout the district to creatively generate support for the Make-A-Wish Foundation. The result of the program was not only to donate significant sums of money for a good cause but also to catalyze a spirit of empowerment for our learners, who experienced how collaborative service can elevate an entire community. One of the notable aspects of Vista's Big Give is that it was initiated, led, and sustained by teachers without any directive from administration.

Leadership can happen from anywhere at any time. Powerful leadership—servant leadership—is rooted in a values-based approach. When one internalizes this idea that leadership is not tied to title or formal authority, it also reinforces the notion that we operate in a living system where each of us has agency to effectuate change. Those who do have formal authority should use it to promote even greater levels of agency within their social system and focus efforts on ensuring that shared values serve to align the individuals within the community around a greater good. Just as this is true for principals and district leaders, the same should be said for teachers in classrooms and for staff members in any role that supports learners. In my view, that includes bus drivers, cafeteria workers, noon duty aides, instructional aides, counselors, office workers, custodians, social workers, maintenance team members, nurses, librarians, and district office

---

[4]More information on this collaboration is available in this podcast from SLI: https://servantleadershipinstitute.podbean.com/e/servant-leadership-action-in-education-with-art-barter-devin-vodicka/.

staff members. Whether through direct interaction or indirect influence, *every* employee of a school district has the potential to be a servant-leader and to effect positive change.

Part of this shift toward leadership without authority is related to the distinction between control and influence. The reality is that leaders do not have control—just the ability to be influential. Once a leader recognizes that they should focus on influence, they also recognize that expanding influence is best achieved through modeling and serving by example, as opposed to focusing on directives.

This approach is not just a theoretical construct. When leaders embody espoused values and generate high levels of trust through their example, others in the organization exhibit higher levels of "citizenship" (i.e., going above and beyond), which contributes to higher levels of organizational effectiveness.[5] Empowering others to act in support of shared values taps into their discretionary energy and activates the latent talent that already exists within the organization.

Being in service to values and to others is the way of an effective servant-leader. We also know from the research on relational trust that competence is a critical element in developing strong relationships and expanding the social capital that fuels accelerating change. In addition to focusing on people, leaders must also be mindful of the systems that shape our behaviors. What follows are some suggestions about how to build the momentum to "get to breakthrough" and achieve system transformation.

## Learner-Centered Leadership

Just as there are frameworks to help us understand what it means to be "learner-centered," it is helpful to have an understanding of the

---

[5]Megan Tschannen-Moran and Wayne K. Hoy, "A Multidisciplinary Analysis of the Nature, Meaning, and Measurement of Trust," *Review of Educational Research* 70, no. 4 (December 1, 2000): 547–93, https://journals.sagepub.com/doi/abs/10.3102/00346543070004547.

kind of learner-centered leadership that took place at Washington Middle. Definitions of leadership are abundant, and there are numerous theories that have emerged and evolved over time. Included in the literature on leadership are models such as "path-goal theory" (in which the leader's job is to clear the path for others to achieve a goal) and the "great man" approach (which essentially suggests that some men—notably taller men—are born with special inherited leadership qualities that are innate and cannot be developed). I find that the most compelling of the models is *transformational leadership*.

Transformational leadership begins with an assumption that all people can learn and grow. The role of the transformational leader is to help others to develop their unique potential. In this way, the leader is in service to others. For this reason, I also believe that there is a strong alignment between the tenets of transformational leadership and servant leadership. Servant-leaders see themselves as being in service to others and to aspirational values.

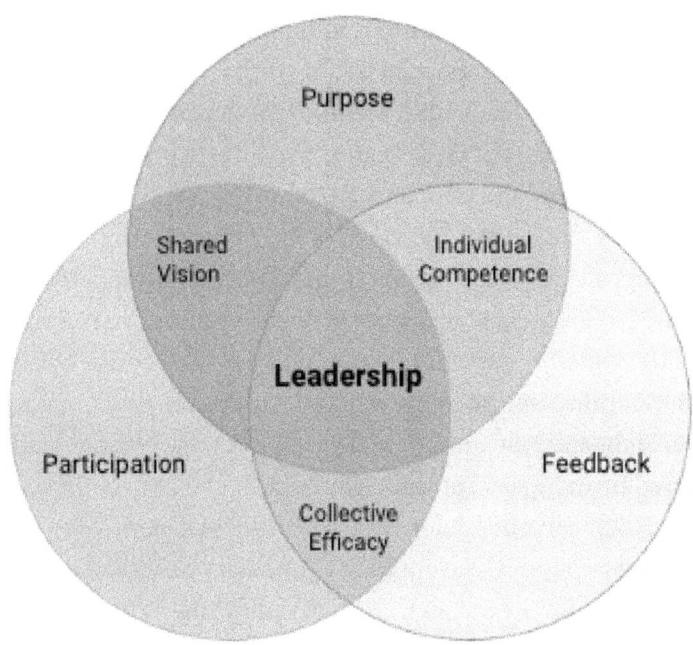

Based on numerous influences over an extended period of time, the best way I can frame learner-centered leadership is to build on some of the living-systems models from Wheatley and Kellner-Rogers and to say that it is the intersection of purpose, participation, and feedback.

## Purpose

In this context, I define *purpose* as having a vision for the future, *participation* as community, and *feedback* as fuel for effective movement. At their intersections, the combined effect of purpose, participation, and feedback is the development of shared vision, collective efficacy, and individual competence. Each of these are critical considerations for learner-centered leaders. Leadership is about a shared vision for the future and purposeful collective movement.

Therefore, I would say that the role of the learner-centered leader is to continually work with others to co-construct a common vision for the future and then to use feedback to fuel the movement that brings the community closer to that aspiration.

One thing that is important to note is that transformational leadership and servant leadership are not role-dependent. In fact, many of the best exemplars of these leaders had little to no formal authority.

In schools, any and all of us can be transformational servant-leaders. I have seen teachers, noon duty aides, library technicians, nurses, assistant principals, custodians, groundskeepers, itinerant specialists, parent volunteers, and students have extraordinary impact on others by modeling servant leadership that elevates others. The most effective administrators I have worked with use their formal authority sparingly and rely almost exclusively on the personal credibility conferred by their servant leadership.

One such servant-leader I worked with was Sam "Mac" McFall, the lead custodian at Calavera Hills Elementary School and also Calavera Hills Middle School, in Carlsbad, California. When Mac retired, he received the longest standing ovation I had ever seen from our students. He was a retired Marine who took exceptional pride in logistics, organization, safety, and creating a welcoming environment for students, staff, families, and the community. His commitment to the school was unparalleled, and his work ethic was inspiring to all who knew him. More than anything, his sincere joy in serving the students made him one of the most popular people on the school grounds. He was such a star on the campus that parent volunteers organized fundraisers such as "Fishing with Mac," where families would donate money to the PTA for the opportunity to hang out with Mac on a Saturday.

In the absence of formal authority, Mac was very much the heartbeat of the school community, and his approach elevated all of us. He exemplified servant leadership. He was a learner-centered leader.

What, exactly, is the learner-centered leader in service to? Simply put, learner-centered leaders are in service to learners. More expansively, all of us are learners and all of us have the opportunity to serve as leaders. We are learning and leading to actualize a desired future state that we have collectively determined is our common vision.

## The Struggle

As we moved forward into devising a plan in Vista, we had to be mindful of our roles as servant-leaders. Understanding the need to change is a good start, but listening to our students, understanding their experiences, and using their input for how we could improve was a critical foundation. That component was key for what came next: the formation of a balanced plan that recognized the interconnectedness of a change process in an educational context.

Understanding the importance of change and developing a plan is one thing; actually implementing that change is an entirely different matter. The inertia of the status quo can be hard to overcome, and it takes a thoughtful and careful approach to make a shift from having a district where ingrained traditions and policies drove the day-to-day procedures to one where engaged, inspired learning was the norm rather than the exception.

In the first draft of the blueprint, we presented a dense, text-heavy plan that included eight strategies, the first two of which were focused on personalized learning. This first draft included detailed plans for actions related to personalized learning, which caused a number of respondents to be reluctant in supporting the plan. We were eager to get into action, and this early version of the blueprint had a quick and aggressive rollout plan that would begin with a significant number of schools in the district. A sequence of activities was established, including professional development sessions, procurement of furniture, implementation of technology solutions, and timelines. Families and staff supported the intent of the plan but had difficulty understanding its particulars. They were hesitant to commit to something that wasn't clear.

We had worked hard to develop these plans, so this initial round of feedback caused some disappointment. But we stepped back and made several adjustments that, in retrospect, turned out to be significant and helpful changes. First, we realized that we needed to visualize the plan in a way that was easier for others to understand. Following the blueprint theme, we called this new representation the "House of Learning." We rewrote and reordered the eight strategies to better capture the interconnectedness of each element. We put family and community partnerships as the foundation of the house, and then moved personalized learning to the roof. This was key to helping our community better understand that we would need to have other components in place to support the shift to personalized learning. Finally, we scrapped our detailed version of the document and determined that we needed to spend time together creating a common definition of personalized learning.

We had done a good job of being inclusive in our approach to inform the key elements of our plan, and we now recognized that we

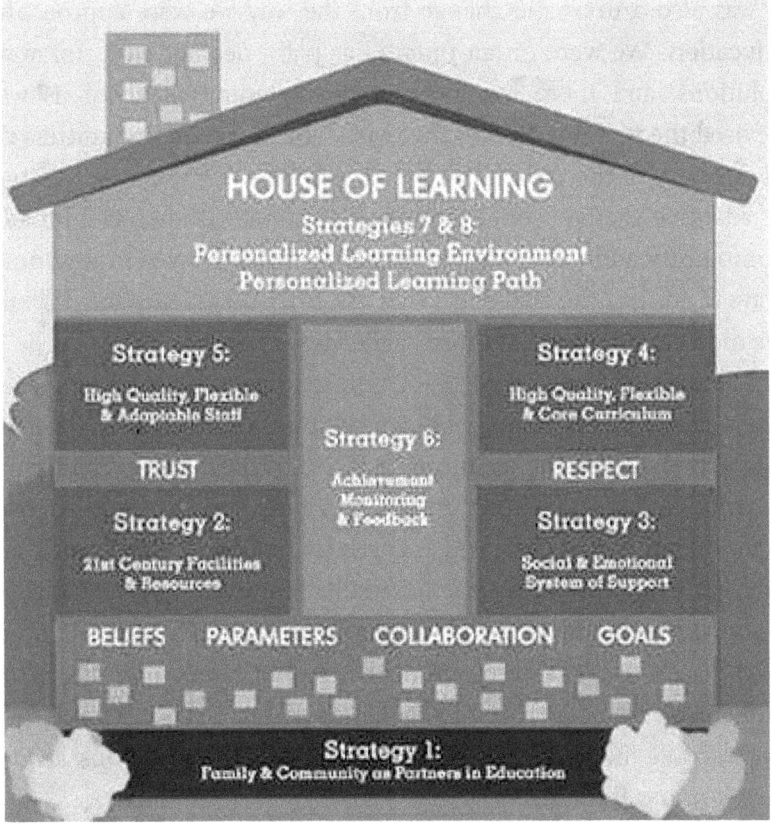

Vista Unified School District: "House of Learning" from the Blueprint

needed to continue including others in co-constructing the implementation of the most aspirational aspects of our approach. People need to be a part of the process in order to continue their belief in the need and potential for the change.

## Listening to the Community

For us, shifting to an entirely new model of learning that would be driven by input from our students was not only a technical challenge;

it was also a dramatic change from the way we were approaching education. We were on an unfamiliar path, dealing with unknown solutions, and there was no expert—including those of us who devised the first iteration of the plan—able to predict or address the complexity of the difficulties ahead. All we knew was that this type of adaptive change would require us to come together as a broader community and collectively struggle with the process to find novel ways to address the challenges that surely lay on the horizon—even if we didn't know yet what those challenges would be.

School leaders, including myself, tend to be more comfortable when they're implementing known solutions or incorporating methods aimed at creating technical changes. In these cases, change can be achieved through a process wherein an expert shares a supposed solution with others in a way that can be replicated consistently and efficiently to achieve a specific result. However, many challenges in our schools today require a transformation of systems through *adaptive change*. This term, coined by Heifetz, refers to solutions that come from the collective intelligence of employees, at all levels, who are learning their way toward solutions together in his book *Leadership Without Easy Answers*.

We began the process of convening various groups of stakeholders to co-construct the definition of *personalized learning*. We immediately began to recognize some tension in our organization as some members pushed for a prescribed, "known" solution that could be implemented predictably, like the rollout of a new textbook. Unfortunately, one cannot standardize personalization. We were running into the limitations of the industrial-age model of school systems. The perceived security and historical dependence of the "command and control" model is at odds with the fact that all individuals have agency and can express that agency in innumerable ways. Active participation from many corners of an organization enhances the change process.

The conversations about learners having agency began to elevate the organizational tensions we experienced, as well. How could we ensure that test scores would rise if we gave students choices? Who would be accountable if test scores did not improve? How could we ensure that compliance mandates would be met, including access to required textbooks, if students each had their own individual pathways? I can't tell you how many leaders and teachers expressed their anxiety at this stage, essentially telling me that the change would not be possible, that it was antithetical to everything that made us a school system.

## Trust and Connectedness

It became apparent that we were facing the problem of how to nudge people along toward necessary change, even when they had reservations.

Fortunately, I had seen a change-management approach that worked. I had originally been introduced to it while completing my doctoral dissertation in collaboration with SRI International, through a study regarding technology implementation and social capital in schools.

First published in 1962, the study, by communications theorist and sociologist Everett Rogers, described a "diffusion of innovation" process, which relied on four elements to spread a new idea: the innovation itself, the communication channels, time, and the social system. Further, Rogers proposed that innovations began with a small subset of the community: the "early adopters" who were more inclined to test out new ideas and be part of the generative, creative phase, when solutions were less clear. The "majority in the middle" would watch and wait, moving only after the first movers were convinced about the efficacy of the new idea. There were also "laggards" on the tail end, who were unlikely to change, even after the idea had been validated and accepted by the majority of the community.

I heard the concerns from our team and empathized with their challenges but also knew that if we were going to be able to meet the needs of the learners we had committed to, we had to change the way we did school at every level. With a clear impetus for change and a vision of what we wanted education in our district to be, I made the decision to begin by engaging with and supporting our early adopters to promote innovation in our system. Based on my understanding of diffusion of innovation, I knew that not everyone

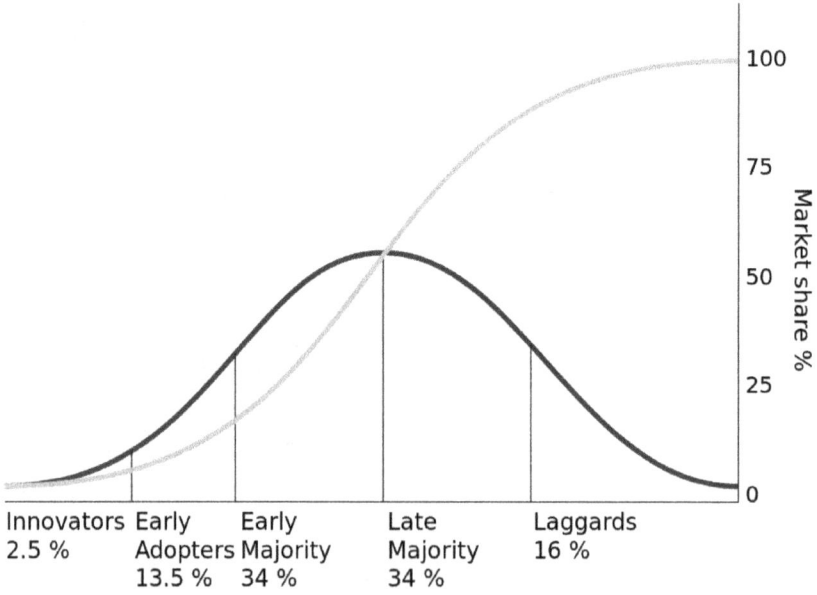

The diffusion of innovations according to Rogers. With successive groups of consumers adopting the new technology (lower curve), its market share (upper curve) will eventually reach the saturation level. In mathematics, the upper curve is known as the **logistic function**. The curve is broken into sections of adopters. Source: Wikipedia.

could make the leap at once. I was careful not to get fixated on those who simply weren't going to be the ones to move first because of their need to "see it" before jumping in. The early adopters, however, were eager to begin. In fact, many of them had been hard at work shifting to learner-centered models for quite some time, often engaging in efforts that were intentionally low profile.

As an example, one of our elementary schools had formerly been a magnet school focused on science and technology. When magnet grant funding dried up, they continued to utilize practices like developing individual assignments for students, even when they were directed to follow a more scripted curriculum. As we began to implement our blueprint, the school was soon widely recognized throughout the region for its success, and to some it looked like an overnight sensation. In reality, what appears to be a sudden breakthrough is often the result of gradual changes that have been occurring away from the spotlight. Some of the teachers from this school who had been quietly using this more flexible approach quickly became leaders among the early adopters in our personal learning effort.

Understanding the Rogers curve helps to lend confidence to the early adopter approach. But I knew that there was also a phase often called "crossing the chasm," the gap between the early adopters and the early majority, which, if not crossed, leaves pockets or islands of innovation that would fail to spread across a school or district. Many effective changes in education have failed to make this leap, and I knew it would be critical to build a collaborative infrastructure so that we would have the interactive space needed for the early adopters to connect and share with the majority in the middle.

## Social Capital

Within every organization, there are individuals who occupy the different categories of the Rogers curve at different times. People are not uniformly early adopters or part of the majority in the middle—it depends on the particulars of a given change at a specific point in time. In other words, a person who is an early adopter for new technologies may also be in the middle when it comes to new approaches with literacy instruction (or vice versa). This is where social network theory and the concept of social capital comes into play.

While we conceive of a school organization as being consistent with an orderly and hierarchical organizational chart, our actual interactions are much more dynamic and complex. A useful way of looking at this is through the lens of *social capital*. Social capital is, essentially, the benefit that emerges through the patterns of our interactions that facilitate the exchange of resources and expertise. Social capital is what emerges from the connections between people.

Put in context, we often think of capital in terms of the conventional definition of goods and money, and sometimes we extend the model to include *human capital*, the expertise that resides within individuals as a result of their experiences and learning. Social capital is the connective tissue between people; it is like the road system that facilitates the flow of resources and expertise. It turns out that high-performing systems have high levels of social capital because collaboration is key.

For example, when I was a principal who was tasked with opening a brand-new school, I found it very helpful to connect with other principals who had been through a similar process. Through their experience, they had developed checklists and could offer reflections that were extremely beneficial. We developed relationships and connections, creating a channel for them to share the resources and expertise they had developed. The connections I formed with the principals did not create new resources but helped me access existing resources that likely would not have been available to me had I not developed those personal relationships. In this way, a social network connection creates social capital that improves performance.

## Crossing the Chasm

In the context of adaptive change, where process and solutions are co-constructed, our early adopters would surely be developing expertise and resources that would be helpful for others. The vast majority of our educators could (and do) similarly benefit from connecting with our early adopters in this process.

In Vista, with the knowledge that a collaborative system would be essential to "cross the chasm," and in a joint effort with our teachers' union, we renegotiated the teacher contract to require additional collaborative time with colleagues every week. In addition to developing relationships, the purpose of this time was to ensure a consistent pattern of reflecting, developing and sharing resources, and building expertise. We partnered with UC San Diego to conduct research on our leadership team and to survey our students, families, and staff to inform continued efforts to expand collaboration. **Isolation is one of chief reasons that educational changes often fail to cross the chasm.** We set out to make the shift as an organization away from individual practice to collective understanding. While this was always a work in progress, the improvements we were able to make over the course of this journey were one of the underappreciated elements of the transformation. We must continue to find ways to connect and learn with one another if we are going to transform a system.

## Connectedness

I was a relatively new administrator when I originally learned about social capital and the significant benefits of a collaborative organization. I then asked myself the question of how to actually create and sustain meaningful connections. After all, my experience had shown that we sometimes engage in a superficial level of engagement with one another—a phenomenon sometimes called "coblabberation"

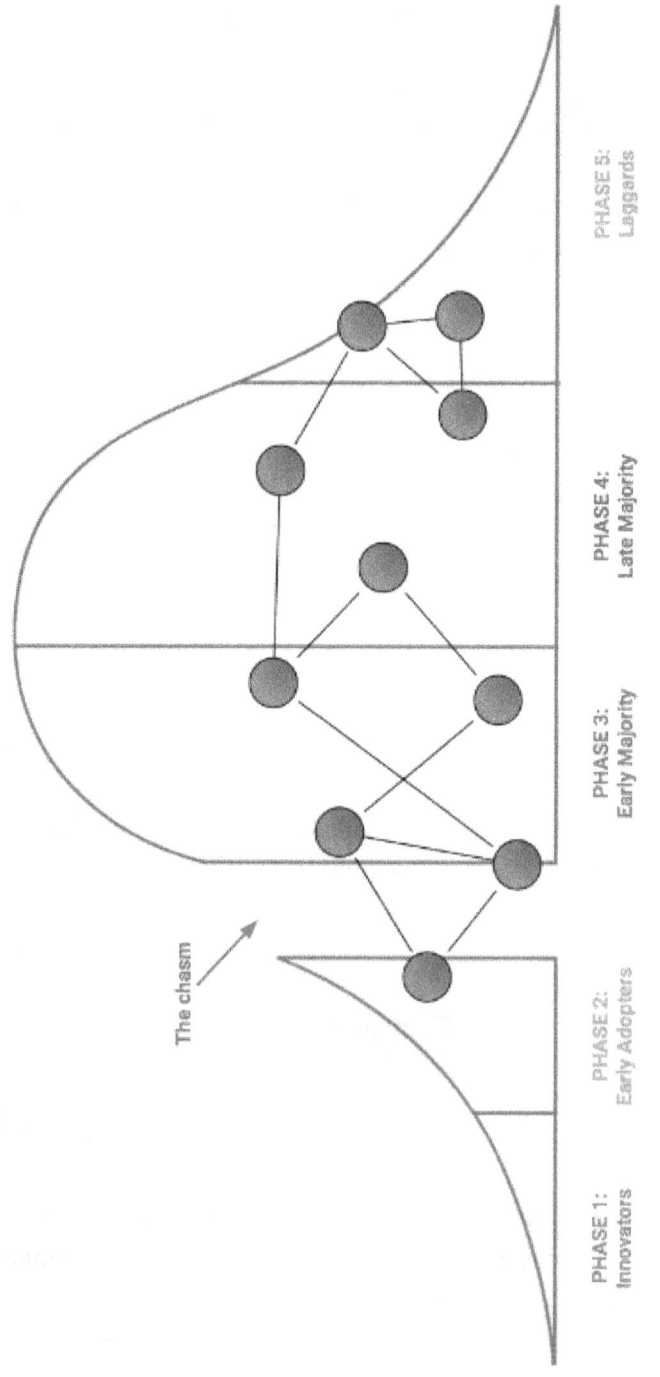

Innovation Adoption Curve and Social Networks

by educators. This line of wondering led me down a path to better understanding *relational trust*.

Relational trust is the key to a strong relationship. My investigations gave me a stronger appreciation of the complexities and tensions that occur when attempting to create trust.

Relational trust is highly situational and dependent on the specific task at hand. It is also dynamic and ever-changing, influenced by every interaction that the individuals involved have had with one another and with others. For example, my wife has a high level of trust in me, and she trusts me with extremely important tasks, such as caring for our children. She also knows me well enough to have formed an accurate impression that she should not trust me to change the oil in a car. I simply have not demonstrated capacity with that kind of task.

## Trust and the Four C's

There are four elements of relational trust: consistency, compassion, competence, and communication.

**Consistency** is equated to predictability. In any interaction there is a degree of vulnerability that occurs, and being predictable reduces the uncertainty of the interaction. This is often extended to concepts such as reliability or integrity, which are absolutely foundational for trust to emerge.

In Vista, the orientation to the Framework for the Future, which included our vision, mission, and values, helped us to build consistency throughout the organization. Adhering to our blueprint helped us have a reliable way to plan and organize our major strategic projects. Use of routines, such as weekly cabinet meetings, is another way to create predictability. Finally, as a leader, it is critical to follow through on commitments, which includes keeping appointments (or renegotiating commitments when necessary).

**Compassion** relates to genuine empathy and understanding. We don't care how much the other person knows until we know how much they care. Compassion is often perceived to exist when there is a meaningful response to a person's unique needs. Further, the research makes it clear that for trust to occur, the compassion must be perceived to be genuine and sincere. Faking it does not cut it in this regard—we have to truly care.

Being responsive to students' needs is one way to demonstrate compassion. Adjusting plans based on feedback is another way to show empathy for others who have differing and important perspectives. Finding ways to bring people together to create community is yet another way for leaders to demonstrate care for others. Finally, slowing down and simply being present and mindful with others is critical for leaders.

**Competence** is tied to the task at hand but can also be perceived based on affiliation or prestige. For example, a student who has graduated from a prestigious school is often perceived to be more competent in their learning than others. Similarly, we can extend presumptions of competence to others based on certifications, awards, and validation from other parties. Competence is a key element of the framework of relational trust in that it shows that being reliable and kind is insufficient to generate trust—you have to get things done and show that you are capable if you want to be trusted.

Making performance quality visible and demonstrating progress toward goals is an excellent way for leaders to demonstrate competence. For example, our Vista School Board agendas included an update on our goals early on in every meeting. This ensured accountability and allowed us to celebrate achievements. Outside validation for our efforts, such as when we were recognized for Digital Learning Day or received invitations to the White House, were also helpful in building positive momentum and community confidence.

**Communication**, finally, is the thread that connects consistency, compassion, and competence. The research on trust shows that the highest-leverage area is actually receptive listening, an underappreciated act in our fast-paced society. Maintaining confidentiality is another critical consideration in establishing and maintaining relational trust.

In Vista, convening community forums and conducting routine surveys were ways to demonstrate that we were focused on listening and taking input. In terms of expressive communication, we implemented a social media strategy, overhauled the district website, and added quarterly newsletters to the community. On a micro-level, leaders should also remember Stephen Covey's habit of "seek first to understand, then be understood," and to ensure that in meetings and informal conversations, the orientation is to first understand the context.

These four elements also exist in opposition to one another. Being consistent and compassionate are often at odds with one another. Consider, for example, the teacher who wonders whether he should make an exception for a student with unique circumstances. If the teacher makes the exception, he demonstrates compassion but undermines consistency. Doing the opposite might convey a lack of regard for the individual and reduce perceptions regarding compassion.

Competence and communication are also at odds with one another. This is a lived tension for school leaders who want to be visible and spend many hours creating communication channels to keep community members informed. While those activities are essential, the task list continues to grow while the leader may be engaged in those communicative activities. In other words, one can do the work, or one can communicate about the work, but it is near impossible to do both at the same time.

The balance of these four elements leads to relational trust. Every leader has to determine their own mix to develop the trust that is key for success in a community of change.

Leading for change requires an understanding of (and appreciation for) the Rogers diffusion of innovation curve, social capital, and relational trust. These are the foundational elements for leaders who are oriented to transformation. A strategic approach that takes into account varied orientations to innovation is imperative. In research terms, awareness and strategic planning that takes into account the Rogers curve is both necessary and not sufficient. In order to achieve necessary *and* sufficient conditions for change, social capital must also be developed by promoting connectedness among the people in the system. Finally, relational trust must be present to create the connectedness and social capital that are required to set the context for the diffusion of innovation.

An awareness of the dynamics of the change process and focused attention on creation of the conditions for meaningful change were important steps on our journey in Vista. Focusing on relational trust, amplifying social capital, and empowering our early adopters were all necessary foundational efforts to move in the direction of systemic transformation. As a result, we made significant progress in achieving our goals, including improvements in traditional metrics such as attendance and graduation rates. Perhaps more importantly, we created an infrastructure to achieve our vision of being the model of educational excellence and innovation. Social connectedness and support for early adopters are absolutely necessary to set the stage for organizational transformation. Without these preconditions, we would not have attracted national attention for the big shifts that we were able to make. As learner-centered leaders, we must attend to relational trust, social capital, and a thoughtful approach for systems change in order to achieve the impact we seek.

## KEY QUESTIONS:

- How might we apply a strategic lens to better implement and sustain change efforts?
- How might we elevate awareness about the dynamics of change and Rogers curve?
- How might we improve collaboration throughout our systems to improve the likelihood of successful diffusion of innovation?
- How might we improve the levels of relational trust in our schools?

Please use the hashtag #LCLeadership and share your responses on social media.

# 4

# A SYSTEM FOR BREAKTHROUGH

"You have to come see this!"

It was late July during the first month of my time as superintendent. The call was from Catina Hancock. She had just been named the interim principal at Vista Academy of Visual and Performing Arts after the previous principal unexpectedly resigned. I had already hired several new principals, and I knew that the pool of candidates was almost nonexistent at this time of the year. In a stroke of good luck, I was able to convince Catina to serve as an interim. I had worked with her extensively in Carlsbad, where she had been a successful principal before making a career adjustment to open a gym with her husband. I am not sure that any other new principal's first call would have been to the superintendent, but I was glad that she made it. Her call triggered a quick visit to the school, and we walked the campus together.

The school facility was in a shocking state of disarray. There was graffiti. There were broken windows. Plumbing that didn't work. Piles of random things all over the place. Half of an old piano sitting in the outside hallway. Electrical problems with the lighting. Weeds that were waist high. One of the walls in a kindergarten room had literally melted from a plumbing leak. It didn't help that it was the oldest campus in the district, with buildings from the 1950s. It looked like the school had been occupied and then abandoned. The students' first day was about two weeks away, and the campus needed a lot of attention.

Catina's call and my visit triggered a series of immediate interventions that included massive cleaning crews and landscape work. By the time students arrived on campus, it had been cleaned up and beautified as much as possible. These improvements were the beginning of a transformation at the school. Catina ended up staying on as principal, and several years later the school was identified as one of just three schools in California to receive the trifecta of earning a Gold Ribbon Award from the California Department of Education, being identified as a Title I high-achieving school, and also being recognized for its exemplary arts program.

The facility problems that we initially encountered were the result of a breakdown in systems. While not every system's state will be as obvious as that of a physical campus, their condition will have a profound impact on the effectiveness of an organization. Each of us who works in education has the ability to influence people and systems. As a result, we can all be leaders. I believe that this is what we are called to do.

## Why Systems Break Down

School leaders are typically conditioned to reduce waste. We frequently revisit staffing formulas, school schedules, and budgets, searching for efficiencies. I recall being thrilled one year that I was able to add two minutes of instructional time per day by eliminating an unnecessary transition, which added up to the equivalent of an entire school day over the course of the 180-day school year. These efforts can make a difference, and they reflect a prudent, efficiency-oriented management approach.

Eliminating waste also means decluttering so that performance quality is more visible. In schools, we are generally really good at creating to-do lists and very bad at creating "to-stop" lists. As a result, programs and practices add up over time, often making it difficult to describe or identify the desired essentials. Even more practically, we often accumulate materials and supplies that were deemed to be helpful at some point in the past and, as a result, our classrooms and schools are stuffed with old, likely obsolete items. Closets are overflowing and campuses become covered with portable storage containers. Spending time eliminating this waste so that more attention can be spent on learning is definitely a smart thing for all leaders to do.

In the case of the campus at Vista Academy, the facility maintenance system broke down. I am not exactly sure why that happened, but there was a huge backlog of maintenance tickets in the queue when I arrived as superintendent. It could have been due to a shortage of staffing, a lack of oversight and prioritization of the tickets, a pressing number of other issues that may have been deemed a higher priority, a failure from school site staff to enter tickets into the system, or any number of other factors. In any event, the system needed to be reconsidered to avoid future breakdowns.

Systems have a profound influence on our behavior. Systems were designed by people, and systems can also change. We were able to make changes to our maintenance system and the way in which we monitored our physical facilities. As a result of our efforts, the state of our physical facilities improved.

## Thinking beyond the Assembly Line

In education, the most pervasive "system" that serves as an organizing principle for schools is the industrial-era assembly line. Is this a system that should be improved upon or an outmoded system that should be transformed? Leaders today should understand that both incremental improvements and transformation are required, and that in order to improve and transform our systems, we must first understand them.

Assembly lines of the Industrial Revolution have had an enormous influence on our education systems. They are the heart of mass production, and they generate enormous efficiencies. In the industrial model of assembly-line production, workers specialize in very specific tasks. The unfinished material moves down the line at a uniform pace, and parts are added to eventually create a uniform, consistent finished product. Our industrial-era schools incorporate the same basic approach, where students move at a uniform pace down the line, progressing from one grade level or course to the next, and workers—in this case teachers—specialize in very specific content, which is added to eventually create a uniform, consistent finished product, in this case a graduate.

Many of the tenets of the industrial assembly line run counter to the core concepts of a learner-centered paradigm. In industrial manufacturing, differences are considered defects. Standardization and efficiency are the primary indicators of success for the traditional assembly line. In addition, the assembly-line approach uses a model that is designed for the production of objects. In a learner-centered model, differences are seen as assets. Agency, collaboration, and problem-solving are the primary indicators of success. The learner-centered model is inherently a recognition that we are human and that our educational approach should be based on a subjective, human-centered model.

So how can we reconcile the tension between our pervasive system of schooling, which treats individuals as if they are parts to be assembled, with the reality that students are human beings who have unique identities and dynamically exist within communities? How can we reconcile the push for standardization with the reality that learning is deeply contextual and that a relevant experience in one setting may be irrelevant in another? As learner-centered leaders, how might an understanding of systems help move us in the direction of a more humane, learner-centered experience for all students?

There is one model that has been demonstrated to be more effective than Henry Ford's approach to the assembly line. It comes from the same sector of auto manufacturing, and it is called the Toyota production system (TPS). Interestingly, while the TPS model is primarily known for its relentless focus on elimination of waste, most of the differences and benefits in this approach are due to its recognition that every person involved in production can drive improvement. This requires providing time and space for the workers to collaborate, reflect, and engage in mutual learning. In the assembly-line model, it also requires a willingness to stop production to bring workers together for that reflective practice.

Under the TPS, any worker can pull a "stop cord" at any time to halt production and draw attention to a challenge. This empowers all workers to take ownership of quality at every stage of the assembly process. You can also imagine that this requires a high degree of trust in the workers, as any abuses of the stop cord can have significant impacts on short-term productivity. The bet here is that by trusting the workers and creating learning opportunities for the team, the long-term productivity gains far outweigh any short-term inefficiencies.

In schools, we don't have the opportunity to pull stop cords and halt production in quite the same way as a manufacturing plant. However, we can learn from this approach where there are mechanisms by which any and all workers can signal concerns that warrant attention. This can take the form of suggestion boxes, anonymous surveys, listening forums, and use of third-party options, such as tip lines for fraud or abuse. When challenges arise, it is often helpful to come together, even with small teams, to reflect and set improvement plans together.

## Pulling the Stop Cord

When a system breaks down, we need to pull the stop cord. One example comes to mind from my days as an elementary principal at a new school. We were having significant discipline issues on the handball courts, and a teacher on duty decided to put a stop to the handball games until we could establish a better approach. We convened a small group of influential students to review and define the rules, which we then posted in several prominent locations. Involving the students in this case was vital in setting the conditions for improvement (we had no idea what their invented terms such as "rainbows" and "bouncies" meant until we worked on common definitions!). By pausing the activity, reflecting, and resetting, we were able to create a foundation for greater productivity, albeit in a recreational setting. We had very few handball problems after this experience, and we can emulate this process with other problems we encounter in our schools and districts.

Reducing waste, providing time and space for employees to reflect and learn, and making performance quality visible are all advisable strategies that can result in positive, incremental improvements. In particular, valuing reflection as an important way to promote learning of the "workers" is something we should do more of in schools.

Learner-centered leaders should not take the status quo as an immutable given. We should ask ourselves where we need to "pull the stop cord," bring people together, create shared context, and set new plans. In a sense, that is exactly what we do when we periodically step back and set (or reset) the vision, mission, values, goals, roles and responsibilities, and strategic plans that comprise the elements of a comprehensive Framework for the Future.

## Shifting from the Industrial Model

What would happen if we embraced a more organic model to reorganize schools? How do these principles align with learner-centered education? What possibilities for individualization, differentiation, and customization would develop? How would customization and allowing for learners to drive their experiences affect student achievement?

There is a model known as *cellular manufacturing* that attempts to bring principles of living systems into the process. This is the closest analogue I have found to a more human-centered approach that also builds on the efficiencies found in assembly lines. In cellular manufacturing, instead of workers specializing on one task, they are organized into cross-functional teams and given the responsibility to bring a product all the way to completion. In these "cells," each team is provided with an abundance of information, and they are accountable for outcomes instead of process. This provides for more ownership, more rapid learning, and also for customization that builds on the strengths of each team.

What if we took the principles of cellular manufacturing and a living-systems model and applied them to an educational context? In my experience, this is where transformation occurs. For learner-centered leaders, the implications are significant when we move from an industrial-factory-model paradigm to a more human-centered approach to education.

*Focus on consistency and control → Focus on adaptability and flexibility*

Schools are currently in a period of transition. Consistency is presently mandated through standards and testing, while families and students expect that their individual needs will be met through differentiation and customization.

In a learner-centered model, adaptability and flexibility of the learner will be emphasized. Eventually metrics for success will shift from standardized testing to more holistic views of learner success.

*Homogeneous groups to promote efficiency → Mixed groupings*

Students have traditionally been tracked or grouped by ability. One argument in favor of homogeneous tracking is that it must be done to make it easier for the teacher. The new model implies that there are benefits to heterogeneity, and that the process should be based on the needs of the customer (families) instead of the convenience of the worker (teachers).

In a learner-centered model, the grouping of learners varies based on the learners' dynamic needs. Diversity is celebrated, and differences among groups of learners are seen as a benefit for learning.

### *The educator specializes in a specific function → Cross-functional work is integral*

Teachers have conventionally specialized in a grade-level or subject area. The new model implies that teachers should be able to perform with any student composition or subject area. Given potential changes in student demographics, it makes sense that the potential for customization increases when teachers can perform a variety of functions.

In a learner-centered model, generalist educators will be highly valued, particularly those who are able to connect their learners with specialists who have deep domain expertise.

### *Individual Work → Teamwork*

Think about the phrase "self-contained classroom." Isolation was the norm under the old paradigm. The new model suggests that teamwork is the best way to meet the individual needs of many students.

In a learner-centered model, educators will operate in teams. There will be no "self-contained" classrooms, as mastery learning will be valued, anytime and anyplace.

*Educators are given information on a "need-to-know" basis →Access to abundant information*

Traditionally, administrators determined decisions about personnel, school finance, and curricular issues. The new model suggests that the entire staff needs to have access to information to allow for more localized decision-making. Customization is predicated on knowing the needs of the customer and the resources available within the organization.

In a learner-centered model, access to a variety of experiences and information helps learners to better understand themselves and the world. Openness is a core tenet of this approach.

*Workers are told what to do, how to do it, and when it needs to be done → Workers collaborate with team members to decide how to meet performance deadlines*

In the traditional model, detailed and sequential curricular materials virtually scripted the work of the teacher to optimize control and consistency. The new model implies that performance outcomes need to be clear and that teams must work together to creatively meet the needs of individual students. Different teams may develop different procedures and use different resources to get the job done.

Learner-centered models recognize that the world increasingly relies on agency and self-management. With scaffolding and support, teachers and students will work together to co-design and implement plans to succeed.

*Products must meet consistency specifications. Deviations from the norm are considered to be problems → Products must meet performance expectations of customers. Deviations from the norm (customization) are considered to be beneficial*

In the traditional assembly-line model, all of the products were identical. For example, every Model T was black. The new model encourages and supports the notion that outcomes can and should be individualized.

Learner-centered education values and celebrates uniqueness and diversity. Our differences fuel innovation, creativity, and greater opportunities for growth.

*Efficiency → Quality*

At the core, the industrial model of mass-produced education is organized to be efficient. It was never designed to be learner-centered, as the primary goals were to align with the needs of an industrial society in which workers needed to learn how to be compliant and to organize efficiently to maximize production.

The context now is very different. Having a system that is efficiently oriented to producing "standardized" outputs in a dynamic, rapidly changing world makes no sense. We need to be oriented to the quality of the experience in order to ensure that learners know themselves, see themselves as being full of possibility, and are actively contributing to a community of mutual support.

## Putting the Pieces Together

These shifts represent some practical, discrete steps that can be taken by leaders to improve efficiency through incremental progress and also promote transformation. Empowerment of teams of workers, access to information, and valuing diverse inputs to inform learning are important ways to promote transformation of our systems. Not coincidentally, the notion of promoting collaboration and teams is highly congruent with the need to focus on relational trust, social networks, and social capital. Providing access to information makes sense when we consider leadership from the perspective of agency

## A SYSTEM FOR BREAKTHROUGH

and choice. Distributing authority to teams who are close to the work is a logical approach in the context of adaptive change.

While these may seem on many levels to be common-sense, irrefutable concepts, the reality is that any change can create anxiety and can be seen as a threat. Messaging these adjustments can also be seen as a critique of the past, which can lead to defensive sentiments. As a result, I have become an advocate for integral thinker and philosopher Ken Wilber's description of evolutionary change: "include and transcend." In biological evolution, this approach has led to the development of extraordinarily complex organisms and reflects a fundamental principle that growth occurs not through destruction (i.e., of the past) but by including and transcending to new identities that subsume what already existed. This can be done in practical terms by honoring the past, recognizing that decisions were made based on the best information available at that time, and presuming positive intent with any and all organizational legacies.

The reality of our current context is that leaders are accountable for incremental improvements, and yet many of us also feel the moral imperative to catalyze transformational change. The other reality of our current context is that leaders often are under extreme tension, as they feel responsible for both incremental and transformational change. Recall that by "leader," I am referring to those with and without formal authority—this includes superintendents, district administrators, site administrators, teachers, and classified staff members that function as servant-leaders by embodying values that elevate others. In order to do both, we must also understand that we are organized formally into hierarchies and informally into networks.

To drive both incremental and transformational change, the best approach I have seen is articulated by John Kotter's "dual operating system." Kotter suggests that organizations should strive for incremental improvement through the traditional, structured hierarchy that creates a sense of order, while simultaneously nurturing an informal social network that relies on a "volunteer army" that operates interdependently to address complex and adaptive challenges. With both of these approaches in place, Kotter believes that organizations can achieve the balance of efficiency and adaptability required for ongoing success.

## Pushing for Speed: Sprint Cycles and Failure

We attempted to embrace the dual operating system in Vista by engaging in "sprint cycles" with our leadership team. The idea was to emulate the sprint cycles used in software development by rapidly rotating through short periods of planning, implementing, and reflecting. Based on research about optimal group size, we arranged our administrators into random groups of five to seven leaders who self-organized to generate plans over a two-week period tied to a district goal, and who then spent two weeks implementing the plans, then two weeks reflecting, before shifting back to another cycle of planning, implementation, and reflection. At the reflection point of each two-week period, one representative from each team would meet to share and learn from one another, to promote collective learning across the district.

The first time we went through the sprint process, we focused on improving literacy outcomes for learners. There were several amazing surprises in the process. First, the random groupings put leaders into proximity with others they may not have known well. We also included our classified leaders in the process, and this meant that a group might include a high school principal, a food service manager, a middle school assistant principal, the director of information technology, and a curriculum coordinator. Leaders who had been in the district for decades reported that they had never seen these types of groupings before. This resulted in new relationships that would be helpful for other collaborative efforts in the future. In addition, by focusing the sprint cycles on a literacy goal and asking all leaders to contribute to this outcome, we fortified the notion that all of us, regardless of our specific responsibilities, were accountable for the success of our learners. Some of the best ideas came from unexpected sources, and the cross-functional composition of the teams reinforced the benefits of diversity of perspectives in our collaborative efforts.

Initially, the teams struggled with the short duration of each cycle—particularly the two-week implementation period. We are acclimated to much longer cycles of attempts at change or improvement, often spanning an annual horizon or at least an entire reporting period, such as a quarter or trimester. How would we know whether what we were doing over a two-week period was resulting in a positive outcome? While challenging, the upside of these brief cycles was to promote a bias toward action and rapid testing of ideas. The reflection period also required the teams to use evidence, which helped to shift our focus to a data-informed approach.

In the first few cycles, I saw high levels of engagement and investment in the process. Teams were generating creative approaches, implementing, refining, and learning from their experiences. We were able to triangulate with other data sources (such as interim assessments and grades), and the initial results were very promising.

The cross-functional teams and short timelines were leading to creative ideas. The orientation to short-term results compelled us to be mindful about evidence and impact. Incorporating reflection and sharing also shifted our culture and helped us to be more open about successes and lessons learned. I was beginning to feel that we were really onto something that had great promise for long-term success.

Unfortunately, it soon became clear that this model was not self-sustaining. Within each group, a small number of leaders were soon doing the bulk of the work and the others were disengaging. Other than peer influence, I had not set any accountability measures into the plans. Aside from the thrill of success, I also had not established any incentives for ongoing involvement. As the year progressed, the diverse and impacted schedules of the participants also became more of an impediment for the ongoing collaboration. The sprint cycles had been layered on existing responsibilities, and I had not taken anything off the participants' plates to create space to sustain the march. After about one semester, it was clear that I had not properly set the conditions for ongoing success and I called a halt to the process.

In retrospect, one of my chief mistakes was to involve all of the leaders in this process at the outset. A smarter approach would have been to solicit volunteers who would be motivated to work through the inevitable challenges of early trials. I should have also been more diligent about incentives, accountability, and relief from other responsibilities.

As an attempt to revive the idea and promote sustainability of the sprint cycles, I proposed a one-year pilot of an opt-in model to the board, which included stipends as an incentive for participating administrators. Unfortunately, I did not time the proposal well and I did not invest enough advance efforts in helping the board understand the benefits of the proposal. The risks were immediately apparent: any leader who operates in a political system knows that compensation increases for administrators is a delicate proposition and one that requires a significant amount of political capital to get over the finish line. I had a mixed reaction from the board and decided to focus my efforts elsewhere. In spite of its potential, this is one of the initiatives that left me with a sense of incompletion.

I share these lessons learned in the hopes that others can benefit from the insights that arise through experience, and also to be clear that the path forward is not easy. Learner-centered leaders must be willing to reassess and "pull the stop cord" on any effort that requires adjustment. It is also important for leaders to demonstrate vulnerability in order to create an environment where measured risk-taking is safe. Shifting to learner-centered education requires changes at the classroom level, school sites, and at the district level. Reorienting from the efficiencies of procedural checklists to cross-functional collaboration focused on outcomes is a massive change that does not happen overnight.

I'm now encouraged to see districts like Arcadia Unified School District embracing the sprint cycle concept and working more strategically to operationalize the process and cultural shifts into their broader strategy. Even more encouraging is to see that Arcadia is part of a small cohort of innovative schools that are connecting, sharing, and learning together to accelerate the collective shift, supported by Next Generation Learning Challenges (NGLC), a national nonprofit that convenes communities of practice to work together on redesigning schools and education. Becoming a learner-centered system is a challenge. The way forward is together, and we must ourselves be willing to be learners on the journey.

## New Possibilities

In spite of challenges, adhering to the key shifts has resulted in transformational changes in a number of settings.

| From (Industrial System—Not Learner-Centered) | To (Learner-Centered System) |
| --- | --- |
| Focus on consistency and control | Focus on adaptability and flexibility |
| Homogeneous groups to promote efficiency | Mixed groupings |
| The educator specializes in a specific function | Cross-functional work is integral |
| Individual work | Teamwork |
| Educators are given information on a "need-to-know" basis | Access to abundant information |

## Arcadia Example of Dual Operating Systems

*Author: David Vannasdall*

Like so many of my peers, as superintendent of Arcadia Unified School District, I sat in the corner office imagining how we might break free from the rigid boundaries of bureaucracy to run the district differently. I had this Silicon Valley image in my head of three employees sitting together in a dorm-like room, making profound decisions about the future of the organization in the same amount of time it takes to finish a latte.

Students are now living in a world where almost everything is personalized to them, from their coffee selection to the news feed on their smartphone. And yet schools continue to look very similar to the industrial-era factory model of rows, bells, and strict compliance: "Don't start packing up until the bell rings, and not a second sooner." Arcadia had just completed many years of districtwide improvement where we focused on building trust, showing vulnerability, cultivating relationships, and establishing a healthy organization. But with the world changing faster than ever before, we wanted to ensure our organization was able to adapt and grow to meet these changes as they emerged. I felt the timing was right for transformational change. And at that point, I was convinced that the only hope for changing our 150-year-old antiquated education system was to begin thinking and acting like a start-up.

So, with the right team assembled, over the course of a school year we became "students" of the most successful new tech companies. We absorbed their network practices, as well as their new and exciting language. Their permission to learn from failure was met with both excitement and fear. Our traditions and processes were quickly replaced with agility and risk taking. We rolled out a districtwide theme of "what if," promoting and prompting staff to question anything and everything, from classroom pedagogy to business services. We reimagined decades-old processes that only existed because "that's the way we always did it." We replaced a three-page, collated form that teachers were previously required to fill out to gain permission to use outside software with two simple questions: Is it legal? Is it good for kids?

During the following two years, this accelerated speed of change was productive in many areas. However, we recognized that cracks were emerging. Traditional lines of communication began breaking down, as they couldn't keep up with the pace of activity. The predictable processes, which used to provide psychological safety and comfort, were no longer constant; they became the source of stress for even the most seasoned leaders. Consequently, there was an erosion in the high level of trust and relationships that existed throughout the organization.

This was not the outcome we were hoping for when we started this journey. It was a pretty difficult moment, as we questioned how we could possibly meet the needs of our students for their future. On one hand, we know that traditional bureaucracy can't change with the times, and we were seeking a new way of functioning that would promote growth. On the other hand, the agility of a start-up seemed to threaten the most basic needs of a learning organization. We were stuck in the binary of old versus new.

John Kotter is a recognized expert in leadership and change management and the best-selling author of *Accelerate: Building Strategic Agility for a Faster-Moving World*. Kotter suggests there is a third option, where the bureaucracy and network can coexist and thrive off each other's strengths. He calls this the *dual operating system*. His dual-operating-system model simultaneously celebrates the need for strong traditional hierarchy, while building a network of small, agile groups that can quickly find solutions in real time. A working theory that brings these two extremes together as one healthy model seemed both inspiring and questionable. Is it possible for staff to exist in a hierarchy, while at times volunteering to participate in flat, non-traditional groups that form and dissolve with each task?

I now believe the answer is yes—and the work to get there is difficult. The fundamental challenge to organizational innovation is the threat it poses to the hierarchy. When systems are challenged, the system naturally seeks out the cause and organizes to neutralize the threat as quickly as possible. What would happen, then, if the innovation is not from the outside or a different department, but is actually coming from the very same system it is threatening? Will staff attack something they have built and own?

John Kotter was gracious enough to engage in these types of discussions with us. We knew his theory worked for enterprise companies, but to our knowledge it had not been applied to an education setting. We came back from meeting with him and shared the theory with the organization, starting with the school principals, who are the ones on the front lines managing changes as they're rolled out. We suspected this would be a situation where "seeing is believing," so we started some "results accelerators"—sample projects for which we gathered the people closest to a specific challenge and empowered them to come together to find solutions with a high level of urgency.

One such problem was around improving early literacy and reading. We charged the principals and staff of our six elementary schools with creating a thirty-day, sixty-day, and ninety-day plan that would include very actionable data accountability. This would mean coming together on a shared problem on the same timeline, but also making allowances for the unique constraints of each campus (from school schedule to staffing). The results in just two months were astounding. In sixty days, they were able to accomplish what would have taken a year or more in a traditional school environment, due to the complexity of the decisions and number of decision-makers involved. Compared to a start-up approach, where innovation was happening outside of the people most impacted, decisions were made collaboratively in a way that enabled rapid movement.

What we are seeing in Arcadia is staff agency—agency to participate in meaningful deep dives with colleagues from all over the district to solve district-level challenges, as well as challenges specific to school sites that have the most difficult student needs.

The magic in Kotter's theory is deeply rooted in research on human motivation. When people are involved in meaningful work around the identification of a problem, they will invest in the solution. There is a high level of control being handed over from administration to the staff who are closest to the issue, or in this case, closest to the students in need. The group of teachers and counselors working on this site-level network team do not have titles or roles dictating the formalities of the work; they are simply the staff that can best contribute to identifying a common challenge and creating a quick plan for achieving a gargantuan goal. There is a high level of urgency, transparency, and accountability for everyone involved.

In Arcadia, we are finding this work to be sustainable, and once established, it becomes part of the hierarchy. The role of the administration is to remove barriers to the work and encourage the team to keep moving toward the big opportunity, one that may have previously seemed impossible but that is happening now that we've embraced the dual-operating-system approach.

| Workers are told what to do, how to do it, and when it needs to be done | Workers collaborate with team members to decide how to meet performance deadlines |
|---|---|
| Products must meet consistency specifications. Deviations from the norm are considered to be problems | Products must meet performance expectations of customers. Deviations from the norm (customization) are considered to be beneficial |
| Efficiency | Quality |

The establishment of the Vista Partnership for Children is an example of the potential for dramatic transformation when we shift to the principles of a learner-centered system. The Vista Partnership for Children was a mixed group that included educators, early education providers, higher-education leaders, business leaders, non-profit agencies, involved families, and medical providers. Together, we reviewed an exhaustive amount of data and information to help identify areas of need. We visited other communities where they had demonstrated the benefits of cross-sector collaboration. As a team, we identified a need to improve early literacy in our community and we set up cross-functional working groups that were oriented around common goals. Early education efforts were expanded, family outreach increased, community partners began to use mobile dental and vision clinics to improve health services directly within schools, and we adjusted district supports to better connect with and support these initiatives. As the superintendent, I conducted monthly literacy leadership meetings with key staff to review progress and support ongoing efforts. As a result of our efforts, from 2013 to 2016, the percentage of incoming kindergarten students who rated as transitional or probable readers went from 19 percent to 61 percent.[6]

---

[6] Devin Vodicka, "Strengthening Early Literacy," *School Administrator* (February 2017), http://my.aasa.org/AASA/Resources/SAMag/2017/Feb17/Vodicka.

At the school level, we incorporated these design principles into the formation of Calavera Hills Elementary School in Carlsbad, California, when it opened in 2002. All students had "cross-age buddies," and families could opt into looping configurations where students stayed with their teachers for two years, frequently set up as combination classes with about half of the students from succeeding grade levels (for example, a first-and-second-grade combination class would have ten first-grade students and ten second-grade students; the first-grade students would continue with the same teacher the following year). The school was honored as a California Distinguished School in its first year of eligibility.

Design 39 is a K–8 school in Poway, California, that has taken these principles to entirely new levels. Openness, teaming, flexibility, and appreciation for uniqueness and diversity of thinking are embedded into the schedules and routines of the school. Students move fluidly between teachers based on their dynamic needs, and learning often extends beyond the classroom and out into the campus or community. Learning exhibitions where students demonstrate their abilities to use design thinking to address complex challenges ensure rigor while also promoting flexibility in how students can demonstrate their competence.

At the high school level, the initial instantiation of the Personal Learning Academy at Vista High School also incorporated these shifts. Teams of four teachers representing each core discipline (English, math, science, and social studies) took a group of students who were assigned to a four-block section with that teaching team. The teachers were given the flexibility to determine the best ways to organize the students, and they used various models based on their learning objectives and the demands of the experiences that were being co-constructed by the team of teachers along with the students. Instead of counting minutes of instruction, we focused on outcomes such as attendance, discipline, student perceptions of school, and academic grades. The dramatic changes—including a 99 percent reduction in discipline incidents, 50 percent reduction of absences, and two-thirds of students gaining a full point on their GPA—helped to set the foundation for the XQ Super School prize that we received.

These successes demonstrate that incorporating the principles of a more humane, learner-centered system produce breakthrough changes that are beneficial for our learners. Learner-centered leadership begins with relational trust and connectedness. Learner-centered leaders also require an orientation to the future and the development of a Framework for the Future to provide clarity on vision, mission, values, goals, roles and responsibility, and a strategic plan. Unleashing the potential of a connected, inspired community then requires the learner-centered leader to shift systems to promote flexibility, provide access to information, support cross-functional teams, place trust in their teams, and establish a relentless focus on quality outcomes.

## KEY QUESTIONS:

- How might you promote incremental improvement (continuous elimination of waste, getting to the root causes of problems, continuous improvement, and making the learning of those involved the central focus) in your learning community?
- How might you promote transformational change (individuals are organized into teams that determine their own schedules, monitor for quality control, alter procedures as necessary, and communicate extensively) in your learning community?

Please use the hashtag #LCLeadership and share your responses on social media.

5

# THE LEARNER TAKES CHARGE

Invariably, the journey to achieve a common vision, embody a mission, actualize values, and accomplish goals requires ongoing input to determine the degree to which progress is being made in order to close the gap between current reality and the desired future state. What gets measured, how it is measured, how it is reported, and what happens with the information are all critical factors that influence the likelihood of eventual success. It is the role of the leader to ensure that progress measures are used to accelerate growth. Based on my experience, the following suggestions may improve the odds.

One of the guiding principles that has served as a foundation for my philosophy regarding metrics and data is to make performance quality visible. We seek to help learners see their learning, own their learning, and then drive their learning. A similar process follows for learners, educators, and leaders with respect to data. In most cases, the first step will be to surface existing information and make it visible for all. As an example, in the TPS model they use dashboards to visualize progress relative to goals. That same practice exists in high-performing classrooms, schools, and districts.

While these early visualizations are a critical first step, ideally the information is portable in such a way that the affected individual or team has easy access to it at all times. I love the analogy of a "digital backpack" as a construct to illustrate both the desired portability while also conveying a sense of ownership. In addition, providing anytime-and-anywhere access is critical to shift away from traditional industrial models of leadership, in which leaders would restrict the flow of information to workers. In a cellular manufacturing model, which better aligns with a learner-centric approach, the more prudent strategy is to provide an abundance of information and allow the learner (or educator) to make sense of it in a way that best fits their unique context.

I have seen a number of well-intended initiatives meant to leverage data fail due to a flawed notion that an "outside-in" approach would have a meaningful impact on learning. In these situations, the original-use cases center on policy makers or educational leaders who are, in most cases, relatively far removed from teaching and learning. The theory of action here is that by making the information relevant for these "decision makers," they in turn will translate and transfer ownership and responsibility to educators, who will then do the same for the learners. This approach essentially posits that the hierarchical, command-and-control model is the most efficient construct for transformation.

It should be no surprise that I have found more success with an opposite approach of beginning with the learner and then cascading out to educators, leaders, and then to a community and policy lens. This "inside-out" model is definitely more aligned with a learner-centered mindset and also ensures relevance and impact for the most important constituent in the process. If we want learners to drive their own experience, the development, design, and implementation of a data model must be focused on how learners can optimally access, own, and influence their outcomes.

## Learner Profiles

Part of the rationale for beginning with the learner is related to an inherent challenge when data is simplified for a broader audience. This compression, which usually takes the form of averaging or some other nuanced weighting, inevitably loses granularity as it gains simplicity. When one begins with a policy-making lens, the data tends to be compressed multiple times before it is intelligible on this broad scale. This phenomenon means that working from an outside-in perspective will require expansiveness as one moves from policy to the learner, which can have unintended consequences that are not always optimal for the learner.

An encouraging approach that may be helpful in considering where to begin with a learner-centered data model is the development and use of holistic learner profiles. This was, in fact, visually represented as the base of the Vista Personal Learning Star. More specifically, we saw this profile as being cumulative, reflecting learners' strengths/interests/values, indicating unique needs, documenting competency milestones, and including a multimedia evidence portfolio.

While we struggled to devise an elegant model in Vista, we knew that we wanted the learner profile to reflect a strengths-based philosophy that would help the learner see an abundance of possibilities. We began to experiment with personal development assessments such as the StrengthsFinder by Gallup, which helps to identify individual strengths. We also used the Strong Interest Inventory from CPP, which helps to create insights about individual interests for consideration of potential careers. We asked students to do writing projects about their family history, and in some cases, these turned into amazing video documentaries. The main idea here was that we wanted to encourage students to see themselves as capable contributors.

I recall walking into a classroom at one of our middle schools while the students were engaged in a writing project. As I was speaking with one of the students, a classmate came over to ask for her

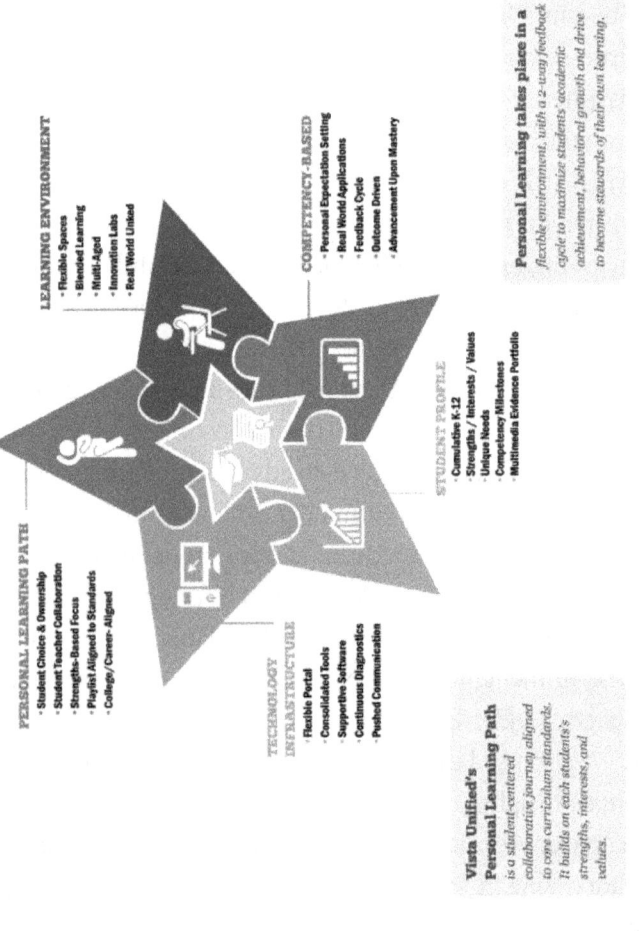

Vista Unified School District Personal Learning Star

help. This classmate specifically sought her out because they needed a creative solution and they knew she had self-identified ideation as one of her strengths. I found out later that the student with ideation capacity had struggled on many traditional academic measures and had developed a poor self-perception over time. By shifting to a strengths-based model, she was beginning to see herself as a positive contributor and her level of engagement in the learning process was already beginning to improve.

Odyssey STEM Academy, an innovative high school in Paramount, California, visualizes learner profiles in common spaces using poster paper and Post-it Notes. Similar to our approach in Vista, their profiles include strengths and interests and also expand into vocational values and careers. As indicated in both models, these learner profiles are frequently qualitative and include information beyond the attendance, grade point averages, and test scores that are conventionally referenced in education.

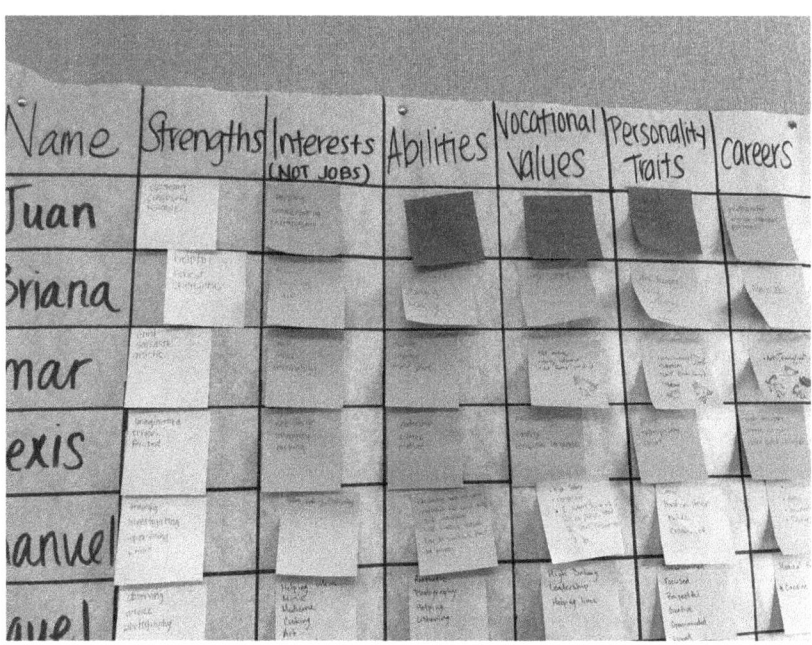

Odyssey STEM Academy, Paramount, California, 2018

## Odyssey STEM Academy: Charting a New Course for America's High Schools

*Authors: Keith Nuthall, principal, and Becky Perez, academic dean*

Nestled among Southern Los Angeles County communities, Paramount Unified School District (PUSD) was a one-high-school town with a long history of serving nearly five thousand urban youth. The community nearly bleeds maroon and white, and alumni greet each other with a handshake and the motto "Once a pirate, always a pirate."

At the same time, our superintendent recognized that a Paramount Unified diploma holds diminishing currency with colleges and future employers, and falls short in ensuring active participation in our democracy.

Today, in most of our nation's high schools, this type of dual reality plays out. At some point in a student's education, critical decisions are made for them about their capabilities, interests, and dreams. These decisions are made by adults in their school and can have life-altering consequences on what students do after graduation and, consequently, throughout the course of their lives. Truly empowering young people as full partners requires educators to:

- Believe in the infinite potential of all learners and trust in their capacity to thrive through an empowering education
- Respect people and show compassion through our actions
- Strive for excellence by seeking feedback, reflecting, and refining our craft
- Demonstrate vulnerability and humility, and commit to individual growth and learning
- Prioritize collaboration based on the belief that collective creativity and diverse perspectives generate our strongest ideas

In fall 2016, Paramount superintendent Dr. Ruth Perez convened a leadership group with the goal and promise to reimagine high school in the district. The team was comprised of PUSD Board of Education members and district and school leaders. One of the very first steps would be to open a brand new forward-thinking high school that could serve as a blueprint for the future. We were fortunate enough to be tapped to lead the new school.

Over a three-month period, the "High School Promise" team moved forward in a fairly predictable fashion by touring innovative high schools throughout California. School visits ended with common themes and unique characteristics handwritten on seemingly a thousand flip charts. This initial phase identified three nonnegotiables:

- Approach: learning will focus on STEM
- Access: there will be no learner entrance requirements, such as grades or behavior
- Address: the new school will occupy a former elementary school site with twenty-four portable classrooms

The High School Promise team was expanded by adding student, family, and university representation, and a founding principal, all of whom brought new perspectives and richness to the dialogue. The larger fifty-plus-member Odyssey design team engaged in a year-long iterative design process, examining perspectives, research, and rationale for key decisions represented in the flip charts from visits to innovative high schools.

The team analyzed current practices and expectations in Paramount Unified and crafted a school mission, values statement, design principles, and graduate profile tailored to our community. This living document answers key questions and guides present and future decision-making. These ideals serve as our North Star at Odyssey STEM Academy. They guide our most difficult choices and align us to our mission:

> Empowering learners by awakening their curiosity and passion to transform themselves and the world.

These words are strategic and all lead back to one of the fundamental differences between Odyssey and most other schools: each student is truly at the center of and is driving his or her own learning journey. The design and approach at Odyssey are radical departures from the more traditional model that (out of habit or perceived necessity) places the teacher at the center of learning, with students filling in around them.

Visitors to Odyssey STEM Academy arrive eager to experience a new high school that is intentionally designed around students' interests, voices, and choices. They learn about our school through storytelling with a freshman, which often results in exchanging contact information to stay in touch.

Blue is a charismatic young man who speaks with his hands. On a rainy day in March, a visiting superintendent asked Blue to partner with him for the morning. Over the next couple hours, they exchanged heartfelt stories about their passions in life and future aspirations.

Blue described his current internship at a local vintage Volkswagen restoration shop and expressed gratitude toward his mentor, Manny. After all, Blue is fourteen years old, and his quest to intern with a construction or mechanic mentor was met with rejection by over twenty businesses before he connected with Old Speed VW Restoration. Blue thought the internship design was cool. Twice a week, for eight weeks, school was off-campus from 4 to 8 p.m., and Blue spoke with pride about persistence.

Our guest prompted Blue to paint a picture of a typical school day on campus. Blue described tackling a design challenge in our Idea Lab to create a tool or robot to help a species thrive under duress in a harsh underwater world. Working as an apprentice under an architect fellow from NuVu Studio, Blue and his partner

Maricruz identified the green sturgeon as their species to protect. They problem-solved, tweaked, and prototyped early and often. Each time, they documented and explained their choices through sketches, photographs, and blog reflections.

Blue then explained how the Idea Lab project connects to Humanities Studio, where he reads, writes, and participated in a Socratic seminar, where students grappled with the ethics and ramifications of both widespread alterations to the biosphere and the idea that humans can and should act to help plants and animals protect themselves. During STEM Studio, Blue explored how circuitry, motors, and coding work together, skills he would need to program his own machine.

Each trimester would end with students defending their learning across all disciplines by presenting their designs and telling their "soul story"—a reflection of their growth and struggles through a portfolio presentation. Blue was open and honest about his struggles in mathematics and spoke with confidence about his improvement in writing. Reflection, revision, and redemption are essential to academic and personal development.

When looking at a student's work, Elliot Washor, cofounder of Big Picture Learning, is fond of asking a curious question: "Is this your work, or is this schoolwork?" Visitors to Odyssey are given this question to ask, and when the superintendent posed it to Blue, he reflected, hesitated, and responded, "Sometimes it's my work."

Blue was learning to manage his own learning, and we at Odyssey were learning how to co-construct learning experiences that would place all students at the center of their own learning.

Establishing and nurturing equitable, learner-centric opportunities is complex, messy, and challenging. We are learning that seemingly inconsequential decisions can tip the scale toward traditional, educator-centric schoolwork. These decisions often surface in response to concerns about students' progress toward learning goal outcomes and can result in a return to assessing

> content-based, discrete skills and knowledge. In these difficult times, our North Star guides us back to what matters most.
>
> Intentional structures and tools empower students to set goals and monitor their own learning journey. Altitude Learning is one such tool. Through Altitude Learning's platform, students are actively linked to their families, changing their roles from passive bystanders to active participants in their child's academic and developmental growth.
>
> Most importantly, our culture places our students' hands back on the tiller, reminding Team Odyssey of our role in the learning process: trusted advisors in our scholars' journey.

The importance of learner profiles is reinforced when one takes a living-systems view on education. In an industrial model, all "parts" (i.e., learners) are presumed to be the same, each receiving the same standardized treatment as they move down the conveyor belt. In a living-systems view, individuals are seen as unique and as having agency to act. These agents make choices through their own lens, and one of the primary motivators for decision-making is based on identity. Given the strong influence of identity, it is important that a postindustrial system of teaching and learning provide opportunities for self-reflection, self-reference, and self-awareness.

## Measuring What Matters

While the general concept of making performance quality visible is a recommended strategy for any endeavor, it is also critical to be mindful about which measures are identified and utilized. As the maxim indicates: "What gets measured gets done." As noted by University of Kansas School of Education professor Yong Zhao, there are also tradeoffs or "side effects" that are often underappreciated when we emphasize particular outcomes. For these reasons, it is important to step back and consider how to create a balanced set of metrics that can serve to promote holistic and meaningful improvements.

In terms of student achievement, I won't belabor the flaws of the most prevalent metrics of the industrial era of education, but I will point out that standardized testing and grade-point averages are not sufficient to meet the needs of our postindustrial time. Standardized testing has an enviable simplicity in terms of reporting and with respect to generating comparisons to samples of students through norm-referenced percentile rankings. But, in addition to having the "side effect" of narrowing the curriculum to subjects like language arts and mathematics, a fundamental irony of our emphasis on standardized tests is that the acceleration of artificial intelligence is leading us to a place where robots are increasingly outperforming humans on these multiple-choice tests. If robots are better at doing these types of tasks, we can be sure that the jobs of the future that rely on identifying the best answer out of a preselected set of options will be automated. This means that we are currently building capacity in our students for what will be an obsolete market, and in the process, we are sacrificing the opportunity to focus on more important elements, such as the cultivation of enduring habits and skills.

Grade point averages are another tantalizing metric, due to their simplicity and the significant emphasis placed on this outcome in the admissions process for higher education. While there are some studies indicating that GPA does hold some long-term predictive values, a deeper look illustrates that the construct itself has very little to do with learning and instead serves as an indirect proxy for other variables—such as work habits and persistence—that may have relevance in other areas of life.

Grade point averages are founded on two completely arbitrary and invented foundational elements: grades and *Carnegie Units*, equivalent to 120 hours of class time. Our established A–F model of grading, which relies on well-known percentages (90 percent and above is an A, 80–89 percent is a B, etc.), was invented in the late 1800s and appears to have its origins in higher education, and more specifically at Harvard. I mention this because, while we often presume that use of letter grades is a given, it was invented by educators and can be reinvented by educators. The reality is that we use grade point averages due to convention, policies that we also invented, and the notion that "we've always done it this way."

Grading practices vary wildly among teachers, and one of the key reasons for this variation is that a percentage score omits the critical variable of the complexity of the tasks. For example, is it better to get 100 percent accuracy on a test that measures second-grade content (which would equate to an A), or 75 percent accuracy on a test that measures fifth-grade content (which would equate to a C)? The percentage and corresponding letter grade do not illustrate the rigor of the task.

Letter grades and percentage weighting also rely on the deeply flawed practice of averaging results over a period of time. This approach punishes learners who begin a course with limited background knowledge and masks trends that are potentially revealing in terms of mastery. In addition, these averages often overweight tasks, such as homework, that are often indicators of compliance and task completion as opposed to demonstrations of knowledge competence.

Now it gets worse. We take these flawed averages for particular courses and average them across courses without questioning the assumptions behind the separation of disciplines, the sequence of courses, and the ways in which we decided to distribute time and "credit" across these courses. This is another invented approach that can be reinvented. The constraints of our industrial-era system were designed and implemented by people, and people have the opportunity to redesign and reimplement new systems.

First, we should take note of our current approach of separating English, mathematics, science, social science, physical education, world languages, career technical education, and the arts into separate disciplines. This segmentation is rooted in a mechanistic notion that by reducing a whole into its parts and then understanding the parts, one will develop meaningful understanding. Further, there are deep-rooted philosophies of education that emphasize a broad, "liberal arts" experience to prepare well-rounded critical thinkers. There are benefits to diving deep in particular areas, and I applaud the aspirations of these foundational philosophies. But one fundamental problem is that these assumptions have institutionalized an approach that was conceived before we had brain-based research about how we actually learn. While it turns out that we have some areas of specialization, for the most part our brain processes in an interconnected fashion. As a result, discrete, separated experiences are often housed in short-term memory, which does not transfer to our long-term memory. This is why first-year college students forget up to 60 percent of the material they learned in high school.[7] The learner memorized enough information using short-term processing, and the brain conveniently deleted that information as soon as it was no longer relevant. In contrast, interconnected experiences and "deeper learning" tend to be stored in long-term memory and result in more enduring understanding.

Our improved understanding of how the brain works illustrates why interdisciplinary learning is so important, and yet we continue to use a course of study that was developed by the Committee of Ten educators back in the late 1800s, whom the National Education Association tapped to recommend a standardized high school curriculum. In addition to the lack of more integrated learning experiences, there were a number of assumptions made in the original sequencing of courses that we also often presume are based on solid foundations.

---

[7] J Baulkman, "First-Year College Students Forget up to 60 Percent of Material They Learned High School," *University Herald*, June 25, 2014, Students, https://www.universityherald.com/articles/10125/20140625/first-year-college-students-forget-up-to-60-percent-of-material-they-learned-high-school.htm.

Educators are often shocked to find out, for example, that the logic behind sequencing high school science courses is rooted in what was perceived to be relevant in 1894, when most students only completed two years of high school. I have yet to find, for example, a good explanation for why most math sequences go from Algebra to Geometry and then to Algebra II. Despite the lack of grounded research in this order and the lack of any significant updates to the course of study in over a century, leaders who have attempted to adjust these courses have often encountered significant resistance from both educators and families.

Even more bewildering is the way that we allocate time to these courses. Just about every high school in the US awards five credits for a ninety-hour course, and I have found very few educators who understand how we came to organize ourselves into this model.

To be blunt, it is astonishing that now millions of learners are organized into courses of fixed duration, regardless of the content, the variation of learners, and whether students are actually demonstrating any mastery. We award "credit" based on seat time and further associate funding streams with this seat time (i.e., attendance). This foundational building block of our entire secondary system turns out to be a house of cards that has somehow withstood decades without any serious reconsideration or modification.

It is time for a change.

## Postindustrial Measures of Success

Traditional academic knowledge is absolutely imperative, and we should maintain the goal that all learners master foundational skills in literacy, language, mathematics, science, social studies, and the arts. The brain is interconnected with our physical system, and health and wellness are essential areas of emphasis in a comprehensive education. Now is the time to transcend our industrial system of measures and go beyond test scores and grade point averages. Now is the time to think holistically about what really matters in our postindustrial, high-tech, globally connected age.

Measuring the right things makes a difference. For this reason, one of my recent projects has been to develop a model to provide a framework for modern learning outcomes. This model, called the Impact Framework, provides a window into a possible approach that better reflects the needs of a modern educational system.

This postindustrial system will also require postindustrial measures of success. We can no longer rely on letter grades and seat time requirements as proxies of learning. We are at a stage where evidence of mastery learning is clearly a better way to represent competence. In this competency-based approach, we also have the opportunity to expand beyond traditional academic outcomes and to consider appropriate ways to reflect learner progress through habits and skills grounded in the critical social-emotional learning domains that will be essential for lifelong learning. Additionally, the set of postindustrial measures should reflect the reality that individuals are situated in communities, and they bear responsibilities to contribute to those communities and to the broader social system. We also now have technology tools that can be used to support more complex evaluation.

In short, this postindustrial system should include measures that are situated at the levels of self, others, and community. I will describe these levels using the terms *agency*, *collaboration*, and *problem-solving*.

**Agency** is fundamentally about the learner demonstrating an ability to meet their unique, self-generated goals. While there is a developmentally appropriate sequence of educator-led to co-led to learner-led approaches, the overall trend should be in the direction of learners driving all aspects of their learning, including goal-setting, planning, engagement, assessment, and reflection.

Measuring agency should take three forms:

- Learner self-perception regarding the percentage of time that they drive their learning (self-referenced).
- Competency-based evidence of mastery learning in academic domains such as language and literacy, mathematics, social studies, sciences, the arts, and physical wellness (criterion-referenced).
- Growth and attainment comparisons with other learners. While this has typically taken the form of intermittent standardized tests, this will ideally emerge from the aggregation of daily learning interactions that form the basis of a comprehensive, valid, and reliable data set [8]

**Collaboration** is an umbrella term that is used here to describe the set of habits and skills that are critical for social interaction. There are various models such as the Character Lab set, which includes *self-control, grit, curiosity, growth mindset, gratitude, purpose, social intelligence,* and *zest*, or Stephen Covey's Leader in Me habits, which include *being proactive, beginning with the end in mind, putting first things first, thinking win-win, seeking first to understand and then be understood, synergizing,* and *sharpening the saw.*

Regardless of the model, collaboration is an area where measures of success cannot be represented in a competency-based or mastery model. Developing these habits and skills is an ongoing process. As a result, the measures of collaboration should be grounded in self-reflection, peer assessment, and educator observations that are aggregated over time to illustrate patterns and trends that inform ongoing development. Such measures should encompass both the formal and informal collaborative opportunities that occur through peer interactions. Additionally, these measures can be grounded in frameworks of developmentally appropriate indicators, such

---

[8] Norm-referenced. For more information, see Devin Vodicka, "How to Test for Less," Altitude Learning blog, April 18, 2018, https://www.altitude-learning.com/post/how-to-test-less.

# Learner Outcomes

**AGENCY**
- Strengths, interests, values
- Goals
- Academic mastery
- Growth

**COLLABORATION**
- Global citizen
- Emotionally intelligent
- Flexible

**REAL-WORLD PROBLEM-SOLVING**
- Critical thinking
- Creative + innovative
- Apply knowledge
- Reflective

Altitude

as those in *Essential Skills and Dispositions,* an interdisciplinary framework that was created by the National Center for Innovation in Education.

**Problem-solving** is where the application of self-agency and collaboration results in improvements for the benefit of a community. Problem-solving can be grounded in project-based learning, service learning, challenge-based learning, or any number of models that extend the learning to authentic, real-world contexts. As an example, many schools are orienting students to the United Nations Sustainable Development Goals to provide a framework for contextualized problem-solving. The Sustainable Development Goals were adopted by all UN member states in 2015 as "a universal call to action to end poverty, protect the planet, and ensure that all people enjoy peace and prosperity."[9]

The measurement of problem-solving may also be achieved through expert feedback. This feedback may come through learning exhibitions that rely on the learner to share their journey with experts who can provide meaningful feedback, such as validating impact and suggesting next steps. Portfolios are helpful references for these learning exhibitions, particularly insofar as they offer the right medium for demonstrations over time and the corresponding appropriate evaluations.

The following summary table represents the set of inputs for postindustrial measures that will be required in a learner-centric, postindustrial system that ensures all students achieve their potential. In addition to shifting from a subjective proxy of learning (letter grades) to evidence of mastery, this impact framework also expands our measures to include critical development of habits and skills that result in meaningful problem-solving to improve communities and society.

---

[9] "What Are the Sustainable Development Goals?," Sustainable Development Goals, United Nations Development Programme, https://www.undp.org/content/undp/en/home/sustainable-development-goals.html.

| Agency<br>Goals and Knowledge | Collaboration<br>Habits and Skills | Problem-Solving<br>Learning Exhibitions |
|---|---|---|
| Self-reflection: percentage of time driving the learning | Self-reflection | Self-reflection |
| Mastery of knowledge | Peer feedback | Peer feedback |
| Growth and attainment comparisons | Educator observation | Educator observation |
| Achieving self-generated goals | Patterns and trends over time | Expert feedback |

At the moment, this model is in validation phase and we will soon move to actualize the framework and begin to measure a more comprehensive set of whole-child metrics. This represents the potential for a significant shift in our orientation as we continue to collectively transcend the one-size-fits-all factory model of industrial-age teaching and learning.

## The Power of Story

There is a truism that if you don't tell your own story, someone else will. The likelihood that someone else would capture the essence of your story accurately is much lower than if you were to authentically share it yourself. In a workshop with superintendents in the League of Innovative Schools, Marco Torres, Digital Promise's "storyteller in residence," shared sage advice about how critical it is to tell the story behind the story, in addition to emphasizing outcomes and evidence of impact. He used the analogy of cooking shows and gave the hypothetical example of a show where they simply presented the final product and asked judges to rate the outcomes. This approach, which sadly we sometimes use in education, omits the humanity in the process that engages us, draws us in, creates connectedness, and ultimately helps us to better understand the outcomes.

I am not a big fan of polished media outputs, and I find it far more helpful to elevate the voices of learners, educators, and school leaders who can provide a much more authentic view into the transformational process underway. I have long been an advocate for the use of social media by educators—a view reinforced by the undeniable value of social media engagement in crisis situations, such as school shootings, power outages, and fires—and have spent considerable time and effort helping to create conditions to elevate the voices of others through social media as a way to improve connectedness and transparency.[10]

One of the most impressive storytelling approaches that I have seen is to empower learners to document and share their own experiences. In Vista, this approach was catalyzed by our involvement in Verizon Innovative Learning Schools (VILS), where we were fortunate to have two of the first middle schools in the nation participating in an ambitious project in which every student received a donated iPad with built-in LTE connectivity to provide 24/7 internet access. In addition, the Verizon Foundation provided funding to support a technology coach at each school and resources to launch a student storytelling program through the use of video documentaries.

At each site a teacher was designated to serve as the lead on the student storytelling project, and they were trained by the

---

[10]These efforts began many years ago and are documented in resources such as the TICAL *Social Media Handbook for Administrators* and Charlene Li's "Leadership and Social Media in Education" (https://www.slideshare.net/charleneli/leadership-and-social-media-in-education/14-Learn_with_Monitoring_Tools_What). As indicated in the *Social Media Handbook*, the best approach is to start small, cultivate early adopters, and refine your approach as you go. School leaders are also wise to ensure that they enact appropriate board policies and training procedures to minimize risks and ensure that they are able to focus on the positive benefits.

aforementioned Marco Torres. In a short amount of time, our students were publishing and sharing incredible documentaries about their process of engaging in the transformation of teaching and learning. Soon the videos began to attract local, national, and international attention, enabling our students to visit sites across the nation and even travel to other countries to share their experiences.

## Putting the Pieces Together

Getting to breakthrough is not an easy process. Each of us has the opportunity to contribute as servant-leaders and to take a systems view of the journey. We can increase our odds of success by applying lessons learned to improve efficiencies and expand flexibility in the "assembly-line" process by incorporating concepts such as decluttering, empowering teams, providing information, and making performance quality visible. Balancing the efficiencies of a hierarchical org chart and the dynamism of emerging volunteer networks using a dual-operating-systems approach is another way to promote stability and adaptability.

If we are truly committed to learner-centered experiences, we must also rethink the measures of success that best reflect our aspirations. Many of the conventions of our industrial-age model of education are outdated and now constrain opportunities for meaningful learning. Orienting to agency, collaboration, and problem-solving represents an opportunity to measure what matters and to expand our view of achievement to better align with the needs of modern society.

Along the way, we must remember to share the process and tell the story of our progress. This openness reflects the vulnerability that is necessary to build the trust required to sustain and fuel the journey.

## Vista's Big Give: A $350,000 Grassroots Program Led by Teachers

*Authors: Kelly McKinney, Beth Duncan*

Over the past decade, Vista Unified School District's "Big Give" has raised $346,858 for the Make-A-Wish Foundation of San Diego. The Make-A-Wish Foundation grants life-changing wishes for children with critical illnesses. However, our participation in the program wasn't decided at the district level, or even organized across schools. From day one, this was a grassroots effort driven by teachers.

It started in the fall of 2008 as a call to action by a single, dedicated teacher. She wanted to raise money for the local Make-A-Wish chapter and had the idea of bringing together all the schools in the district, along with the broader community of Vista, California, to do so. Even though only one teacher showed up to the first meeting, a team was born.

In that first year, after many sleepless nights and a lot of hard work by the entire Vista community, we raised $41,000 for the foundation. As years passed, both the team and the scope of fundraising events expanded. By 2014, we featured a golf tournament and corporate sponsorships and presented Make-A-Wish with a check for $78,000. 2018 brought the highest donation total to date, raising over $94,000. Over the years, Vista's Big Give has become one of the largest fundraising events for the San Diego Make-A-Wish Foundation, ranking alongside the Disney Corporation in level of support.

Working from the ground up instead of from the top down presents unique challenges, from leadership to finances. To start, we needed to clear the way to launch the project. First, we met with the superintendent and assistant superintendent of business; next came securing board approval. We wanted to understand district policies and get the board's support. Even if they weren't the ones running the program, the backing of key board leaders opened many doors.

For example, once Vista's Big Give received board approval, sites were allowed to do all cash collections through the ASB accounting system. This ensured there was a safe place to store money and provided a transparent way of collecting funds, selling tickets, and managing all school donations. It also helped when the team conducted work at various sites. Imagine team members, including students, attempting to fundraise at different locations where most people weren't even aware of the campaign. Board approval gave the project credibility. Taking the time to get buy-in up-front helped in countless ways like this down the road.

Next, we needed a team—a large team. We identified passionate leaders at each school. When forming grassroots teams, look for that person who is already juggling a thousand things: they'll either add it to their to-do list or find the right person to help. Many enthusiastic and compassionate teachers, counselors, and administrators stepped forward to serve. Developing student leaders to support a worthy cause is something people have a hard time saying no to.

We learned quickly how to leverage people's strengths and passions. One principal's daughter had received a Wish when she was four years old, as had another teacher's nephew who was battling leukemia. Both the principal and teacher wanted to be involved. We had volunteers who excelled at finances, video production, organizing events, meeting with corporations, or just running errands. Being able to capitalize on their strengths made a stronger foundation.

Perhaps most importantly, we needed a way to raise money for a great cause! Although we had received the blessing of community partners like the school board, Chamber of Commerce, and City Hall leadership, actual financial support was scarce. This was disheartening but didn't stop us. Inspiration came in many surprising ways. For example, we found that the schools with the highest amount of low-income families gave the most, whereas our more affluent schools would either decline participation or put little effort into the fundraising.

So, we challenged each site to have their own local team of students, parents, and staff working together for the fundraiser. This approach was a huge success. We also got into the habit of presenting at the principal's meeting, where we not only asked for support but donations, too! We learned as we went and continuously adjusted our processes. For instance, after realizing people don't carry cash, we were able to obtain a Square device to take credit card payments. And we learned quickly to always involve students in fundraising asks because it's far harder to say no to passionate student leaders.

Overall, we found that our success was based on three founding principles: student leadership, collaboration, and our vision: "The Power of Possibilities."

**Student Leadership:** From the start, we wanted to give students of all ages the opportunity to take ownership in the process. Local college students mentored and worked with our high schools. In turn, high school students mentored our middle school students, and so on. Students shared the message with community leadership and local businesses, speaking on behalf of our entire community for the program. They prepared, practiced, and then presented to anyone who asked. Many times, students would walk away without a donation, but they learned how to accept rejection with grace and professionalism. This life skill is something you can't put a price tag on. Ultimately, every student who participated learned empathy and compassion throughout the process.

**Collaboration:** With all twenty-two thousand students and staff coming together to support the same cause, collaboration and teamwork across the schools were essential to success. High school teams put aside rivalry for teamwork, working tirelessly for our Wish children and their families. For example, one of the biggest events was an all-middle-school dance where twelve hundred students joined together for one huge evening of dancing, friendship, and fun. This event alone raised a staggering $10,000, which was accomplished through student and teacher collaboration. Elementary schools organized together and hosted their own events—penny wars, talent shows, and jog-a-thons.

**Our Vision: The Power of Possibilities:** Ten years ago, no one could have ever imagined that, together, we could raise almost $350,000 for the Make-A-Wish Foundation. None of this would have been possible without the ability to dream big and believe in something bigger than yourself. So, we would empower any team confronting a challenge to make your vision far bigger than you realistically think you'll be able to accomplish. You never know what you can do until you challenge yourself.

## KEY QUESTIONS:

- How might you embrace the notion of being a servant-leader?
- How might you use the principles of the "dual operating system" to promote efficiency and innovation?
- How might you use sprint cycles to accelerate learning and progress?
- How might you make performance quality visible in your context?
- How might you move in the direction of "measuring what matters" and embracing postindustrial outcomes, such as agency, collaboration, and problem-solving?
- How might you tell the story of your process along the way?

Please use the hashtag #LCLeadership and share your responses on social media.

# 6

# MANAGING CHANGE, CHANGING MANAGEMENT

The last thing anyone wants is another meeting. Right? We had curriculum committees, school site councils, leadership team meetings, safety meetings, board meetings, board prep meetings, meetings to plan other meetings, and so on. I don't think we were unique. Schools are complex organizations, and we need to come together frequently to coordinate and collaborate. We also need time to do other work, and I had learned over time to be very careful about scheduling new meetings. Depending on the constituents, there were also collective bargaining agreements that could be very prescriptive about the maximum number of these types of commitments that were permitted.

And so, after we had developed the Framework for the Future, and after we were two years into the implementation of our blueprint, I was surprised to hear that the team wanted something new.

We had hired Gerri Burton from New Learning Ventures to assist us with change management, and she had conducted dozens of one-on-one interviews with team members to inform the next steps in our process. Surprisingly (at least to me), there was clear consensus that our existing structures were not providing opportunities for meaningful sharing of lessons learned as we implemented our new learning model. In response to this input, we formed the Personal Learning Steering Committee, whose members met periodically to connect with one another.

The meeting structure was fairly simple. We included students and opened every meeting with a "lightning round," where one school would share successes and challenges for a few minutes. That generally led to some productive open conversation. We would typically have an external partner, such as Qualcomm or the University of San Diego, share insights from their perspective about changes in the broader context. Then we would engage on one element of the Vista Personal Learning Star, using a start/stop/continue protocol. The goal was to synthesize, capture, and share our lessons learned in a way that would crystallize our collective knowledge and also be a resource to the next wave of implementation.

We were motivated by the concepts in Donald Sull and Kathleen Eisenhardt's "Simple Rules," which outlines a process for reducing the complexity of a major change by identifying a small number of directives to guide decision-making. As a result, we ended up developing common principles like "stop bolting furniture into place," something we learned as we were trying to develop flexible learning environments. These meetings also led us to reconsider our protocols for standardized paint colors, schedules, scaffolds for pathway development, structures for interdisciplinary unit development, and many other key insights.

Importantly, Sull and Eisenhardt indicate that these concrete rules must be created by those who will be implementing the change: "The people who will apply the rules are best able to craft them. They also can test the rules in real time to evaluate whether they are too vague, limiting, or cumbersome."[11]

The Personal Learning Steering Committee continues to this day.[12] The takeaway for learner-centered leaders is that listening to others can inform the development of new structures to sustain and accelerate change efforts. What I learned through this experience is that these types of "guiding coalitions" are actually essential when attempting to transform the learning experience.

## Freeing the Flow of Information

With the reference of a vision, mission, and values, as well as clear, consistent use of metrics related to goals that align with those aspirations, one confronts a number of decisions along the journey. Notably, what happens when progress is not evident? What about when progress is evident in some contexts and not others? When to expand a successful initiative? When to contract?

Here, it is again important to recognize that those in formal positions of authority do not have all of the answers. In addition, often the information that is elevated may not be current or may lack context. It is critical to remember that organizations operate as social systems with complex social networks that are used to exchange resources and information.

While there are benefits to the dual-operating-system model proposed by Kotter, one of the inherent disadvantages of a hierarchy is the fact that information bottlenecks create challenges with the transmission of information. Duncan Watts elegantly describes

---

[11]Donald Sull and Kathleen M. Eisenhardt, "Simple Rules for a Complex World," *Harvard Business Review*, September 2012, https://hbr.org/2012/09/simple-rules-for-a-complex-world.

[12]Recent updates are available at https://www.vistausd.org/cms/one.aspx?pageId=14777051.

LEARNER-CENTERED LEADERSHIP

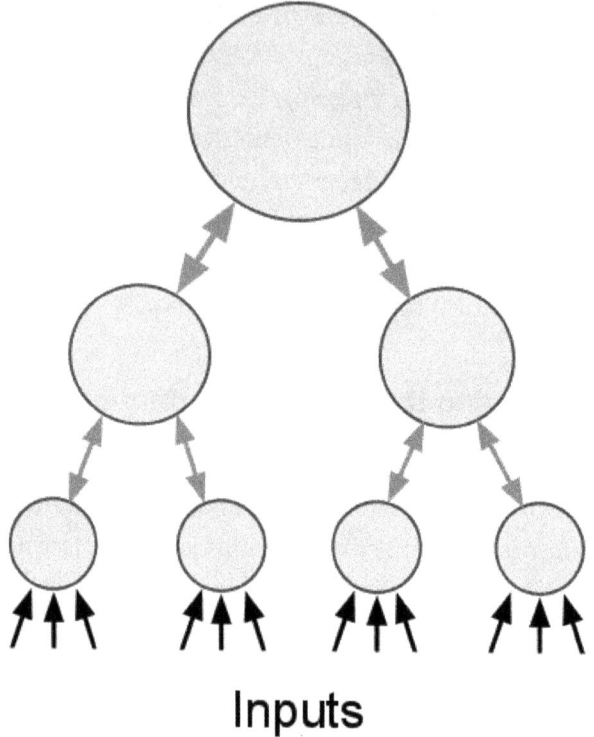

**Inputs**

Information Flow in Idealized Hierarchical Structure

this phenomenon in his classic book *Six Degrees*, with visuals that indicate how the flow of information becomes reliant on individuals in positions of formal authority. This can create delays, miscommunications, and in some cases, a complete absence of information transmission.

When I served as director of curriculum and instruction in the Carlsbad Unified School District, I oversaw all categorical programs and their related finances. As a result, I was an approver on a number of routing systems related to personnel requisitions, purchase requisitions, plan submissions and revisions, and compliance documentation. Many of our systems generated automatic emails to notify me of the status of these procedures. In addition, anxious administrators would often send me emails to add explanations where the systems did not provide for commentary or to elevate urgency around particular submissions. I found myself in a constant state of anxiety due to my own worries about creating a delay or an obstacle that could lead to adverse impacts for learners. I received approximately three hundred emails a day. My survival strategy was to constantly be checking my email—an activity that was at the time more accessible due to the advent of smartphones, which permitted 24/7 connectivity. But this wasn't sustainable.

I learned some techniques for managing my unmanageable inbox, using ideas from Inbox Zero and David Allen's Getting Things Done model. I unsubscribed from lists and deactivated all notifications about incoming emails. This helped.

But the most important thing I learned was that I had imposed an expectation of immediate access and swift response *that was entirely of my own imagination*. Obviously, there was a need for responsiveness, but I had created a model in my own mind that did not align with those of my colleagues. This was a humbling and enlightening experience. It also provided me with an unbelievable sense of relief and soon unlocked a period of far greater productivity for me.

This email example is illustrative of the intricacies of information exchange in a complex system. Other forms of data are shared moment-by-moment through in-person communication, online formats, and social media. There is no way that one person or one leader can possibly manage the abundance, the speed, or the nuance of all these interactions.

The reality that the structures of a typical school system are constrained by these challenges is one of the reasons why it is important to underscore the fundamental problems with centralized, top-down change in a traditional school system.

Dr. Alan Daly, professor of education at University of California, San Diego, notes in his 2010 book, *Social Network Theory and Educational Change*, that our attention to the social dimensions of change and an orientation to social network theory in education is a relatively recent development. As he explained to me, "A social network perspective requires moving our primary focus from the individual (and attributes of that actor) to understanding the more dynamic supports and constraints of the larger social network in which that individual resides." In other words, context matters and a network perspective offers a "complementary perspective and set of methods" that can inform leadership strategies.

In many cases, successful leaders navigate change through their understanding and orientation to the informal social network that exists irrespective of formal titles and positional authority. In addition, we often underestimate how adding new reform efforts can result in overloading the formal structures, and we then attribute the failure of the initiative to the ideas, when in fact the underlying social structures were the primary constraint.

According to Dr. Daly, these dynamics require leaders to be mindful of the need for social awareness, effective collaboration skills, and the use of facilitating, questioning, and active listening. In his own words, "Relationships matter in deep and profound ways to supporting learner-centered leadership."

Given the complexities of these social dynamics, leaders can promote the acceleration of change by focusing on the conditions for success. Many of these conditions have previously been mentioned, including an orientation to relational trust, social networks, the generation, and frequent reference to a comprehensive "Framework for the Future," which includes a vision, mission, values, goals, roles and responsibilities, and having multiple measures that align with those aspirations. Relational trust that grows through consistency, compassion, competence, and communication creates social capital, which is the foundation for adaptive change.

All of these components are critical and foundational. In my experience, they are also less prevalent than we would hope to see in school systems. And yet, even where these conditions are evident, success is not easy to achieve. They are necessary but not sufficient.

There are two primary strategies that I recommend to assist with this portion of the journey. The first is to remain steadfast with the vision, mission, values, and goals, and to also be incredibly flexible with respect to strategies and tactics. The first group represents the future state that one hopes to achieve, which must remain constant, steady, and unchanging. These serve to orient and align individuals, teams, the organization, and the community to a shared purpose and a common destination. After using an inclusive process to ensure that these aspirations are in fact representative of the hopes and dreams of the community, the leader must be relentless in sticking firm to these outcomes.

Simultaneously, the leader must empower and encourage others to be creative and adaptive with the strategies and tactics used to make progress. Moreover, the leader must be comfortable with varied strategies and tactics. This is particularly challenging when we are conditioned by the factory-model approach, which proposes that a one-size-fits-all treatment will result in consistent outcomes. When we recall that individuals are varied, that conditions are dynamic, and that we operate within social systems, it makes more sense to allow for local variations in how to meet the needs of learners. The balancing mechanism that will ensure that these multiple strategies and tactics are actually providing benefits is the consistent use of feedback. This is also where having multiple measures is critical. Additionally, having teams that can make sense of these inputs as a collaborative group is the best way to make sense of the information.

In addition to promoting social connectedness to create the foundation for adaptive change, in Vista I also made extensive use of "superintendent's advisory" structures to expand engagement in the formal, hierarchical decision-making process. Bringing cross-sector representatives together, providing background information, and then soliciting recommendations from the group was an outstanding way for me to be sure that we were using feedback appropriately, and that we were making sense of what were often contradictory signals in the data. These groups also helped to reinforce our value of collaboration and to model the participative structures that I wanted to see at the school and classroom levels, as well. Additionally, I found these groups frequently developed advice and recommendations that were more helpful than what I could have possibly expected to achieve on my own.

Examples of such advisory groups include superintendent's advisory committees to study and make recommendations on our district budget, school attendance boundary changes, and magnet program pathways. The Personal Learning Steering Committee was an example of a cross-sector stakeholder group that came together routinely to share what was working, to highlight successes, and to determine next steps publicly.

One of my favorite stories from the Personal Learning Steering Committee occurred during a conversation about flexible learning environments, where we were discussing how workplaces were increasingly moving to flexible configurations, with stand-up desks, open office concepts, and expanded remote work options. In the course of the discussion, one of our community representatives reminded the group that not all employers had made these shifts and that we needed to prepare our learners to be successful in any setting. Amazingly, it was one of our elementary school students who followed up with a question about how we might promote advocacy so that learners could encourage their employers to consider flexible environments that would meet the varied needs of their team members.

This is a great example of the potential for learners to be contributors, and also an example of the benefits of convening groups with members who have varied perspectives. As Dr. Katie Martin observes in a blog post entitled "Why Are We Still Assigning Homework?," unexplored assumptions regarding the interests of other groups often become institutionalized in ways that are not always productive for our learners.[13] Bringing people together to engage in conversation, to surface questions and concerns and then to determine next steps, is a powerful strategy to expand the range of possibilities.

## Speed Matters!

The key here is to keep learning and to keep moving. Jim Collins refers to the "flywheel effect" in his classic text *Good to Great*. The basic concept is that it takes significant effort to get the flywheel in motion at first, but once it begins to move, it becomes easier and easier to keep it moving due to its momentum.

I would say that the same was true in our early phases of bringing teams together to review data and make recommendations for next steps. It was hard to move at first, and much of the resistance had to do with trust. There were many questions about whether the plans had been predetermined and if the involvement of the individuals was symbolic rather than practical. There were questions about motivation and how dissenting opinions would be handled. All of these were genuine concerns, and it took time for us to demonstrate that the intent was meaningful collaboration, and that we were sincere in our interest to have high levels of engagement and participation from many voices representing all levels in the community. After going through several cycles, things became easier due to the positive experiences that had helped to create that flywheel effect.

Even so, change is always difficult, and facilitators were constantly adapting to individuals at different phases of the transitions process. One of my favorite models to help understand the complexities of the change process is from William Bridges in *Managing Transitions*. Bridges applies his experience as a grief counselor as he outlines three emotional stages that are common in moving through change: the

---

[13]Katie Martin, "Why Are We Still Assigning Homework?," https://katielmartin.com/2017/10/21/why-are-we-still-assigning-homework/.

ending, the neutral zone, and the new beginning. Each of us processes the changes around us at different rates and in different ways, and thus, while some may still be at the "ending" phase, others may be in the "neutral zone," and still others may already be in the "new beginning" stage. Navigating these realities takes time, patience, and awareness.

## Proceed Until Apprehended

Leaders can help to accelerate others through the transition process by remembering the "inside out" nature of change. In my case, we were promoting agency in our students through personalized learners. In systems where self-similarity at different levels helps to build organizational integrity, this requires us to also think about agency for our adult educators, who are also learners.

Just as group participants were initially skeptical about the nature of our "advisory" teams, educational leaders are frequently conditioned to be cautious about change, as well. In Vista, one of our most successful principals was Anthony Barela, the inspirational leader who catalyzed the process of becoming an XQ Super School to reimagine high school while he was at Vista High. (XQ is a nationwide organization dedicated to helping schools across the country rethink and redesign the high school experience.) Anthony had a practice of consulting with me to ensure that he was on track with his approach, and I found myself continuing to tell him that I had confidence in his decisions and that he should proceed without waiting for my consent. After several of these conversations, I finally said something to this effect: "You are an incredible leader, and I know that every decision you make is in the best of interest of our students. I do not want to be an impediment in any way. Please don't ask me for permission to do what is right for the kids. Proceed until apprehended!"

While we both laughed about it, and "proceed until apprehended" became a mantra for the two of us. In retrospect, I am certain that many of the bold steps that led to the creation of the Personalized

Learning Academy and resulting expansion through the XQ Super School Project were made possible by our embracing leader agency to promote speed and acceleration.

I should add the caveat here that, just as an educator adjusts their level of scaffolding for varied learners in a personalized learning classroom, so, too, leaders must adapt their level of support for leaders. And just as personalized learning as a model for students involves use of feedback, connections to standards, and social supports, it is also true that a parallel system for leaders is similarly necessary.

In other words, "proceed until apprehended" is not necessarily the right approach for every leader. With that said, under certain conditions, that type of boundary-setting can unlock what is necessary to unleash potential and to accelerate positive momentum.

When agency is extended to classroom educators, we see similar success. Jenny Chien was an enterprising teacher at Casita Elementary School (within Vista Unified School District) who was inspired to create a "makerspace," a kind of collaborative workspace, at her school. With the encouragement of her principal, Laura Smith, the program soon became a model in the region. Jenny then decided that she wanted to expand opportunities for students to experience computer science, and she designed customized pathways for every learner at her school. She also led an innovative video program for the students. None of these programs were "mandated," nor were they the norm until she demonstrated the incredible impact of these approaches. Many of the practices spread to neighboring schools, and she began to take on statewide leadership responsibilities in Next Generation Science Standards and computer science. Her approach and efforts were recently validated when she was recognized as California Teacher of the Year.

This success can appear obvious in retrospect. Here, I want to emphasize that it was only possible due to the conditions that allowed a talented and dedicated educator to be creative, inventive, and resourceful. Prior to Jenny's recognition, it had been several decades since a teacher in Vista had been a finalist for Teacher of the Year at the county level (which is a precursor to consideration for the statewide award). During that time, we had amazing teachers who were doing excellent work on behalf of our learners, and yet, for us rise to that next level of performance, we needed to deepen the opportunities for our team members to be the best versions of themselves. That occurs not through direct action, but through creating the conditions for such possibilities.

I believe that a new frontier in education is for us to formalize our systems to support educators with competency-based, personalized learning models that are consistent with those we seek to expand for students. We had some early indications through our lab schools at AltSchool that this approach holds great promise. Forward-looking sets of competencies, such as those developed by Jobs for the Future and Council of Chief State School Officers, provide compelling opportunities for us to explore the potential of unleashing educator and educator-leadership agency.

## Moving from Teacher Training to Professional Learning

*Author: Dr. Katie Martin*

A school leader shared with me that, although she felt her school offered ample professional development, she was frustrated they hadn't seen a dramatic shift in the classrooms.

She had hoped to see an increase in students solving authentic problems and using applications for deeper learning experiences. Instead, students used technology to upload and share information, or to complete assignments that looked very similar to the work they had done without technology.

## KEY QUESTIONS:

- How might the use of a guiding coalition and the development of "simple rules" (such as a start/stop/continue list) be helpful to support a significant change effort?
- While holding firm on vision, mission, and values, what are the options to promote connectedness and collaboration to inform adjustments to strategy and tactics?
- How might boundaries be clarified (such as "proceed until apprehended") in a productive way that promotes speed and reduces obstacles?
- How might the systems of professional learning be reconsidered to promote agency, social learning, and competency-based education? How might those systems embrace and model the concepts of a learner-centered approach?

Please use the hashtag #LCLeadership and share your responses on social media.

> I asked the leader to describe a typical professional learning day. She told me that, in every after-school meeting, she showed teachers how to use different apps; in fact, she constantly shared tips on new apps and tools she came across. What puzzled her was that the teachers seemed encouraged in the meetings and even shared their own ideas.
>
> As we dug deeper into why the training wasn't translating into changes in the classroom experience, she realized that her teachers were doing exactly what she had modeled for them: they were using new tools to do the same activities and teach the same content they always had. Although they liked learning about new tools, they hadn't been modeled or used in a way that connected them to student applications for different

or deeper learning.

**Training Versus Learning**

I cringe when I hear the word "training" used to describe educator professional development. Training is something that happens to or is thrust upon people. Learning, on the other hand, is a process of developing knowledge through authentic and relevant experiences. **If professional learning is ever going to be effective in bringing about change for students, it must shift away from something done *to* educators, toward a process of creating a culture of continuous learning cycles and problem-solving.** There is a time to learn new skills or specific programs, but professional learning can't end with information; content is only the beginning.

For these professional learning experiences to move educators, classrooms, and the world forward, a shift away from compliance-based cycles toward empowering teachers to drive their learning is critical. Imagine this same cycle, but instead, teachers have opportunities to experience new models of learning and shift their thinking about what is possible in the classroom. Based on new experiences, teachers work together to select goals and research what works in their classrooms with their learners. They determine the best evidence to gather and analyze based on their goals. Teachers collectively provide and receive peer feedback and support to improve, based on the shared vision, their goals, and the needs of their learners. The following cycle was created to ensure that the vision and goals for learners remain the driving force for job-embedded cycles of professional learning.

To meet the needs of learners in your classrooms and move forward (not just get better at what has always been done), here are four questions to assess your professional learning cycles:

- What is the vision for learners?
- How do professional learning experiences model the type of learning you want to see in the classroom?

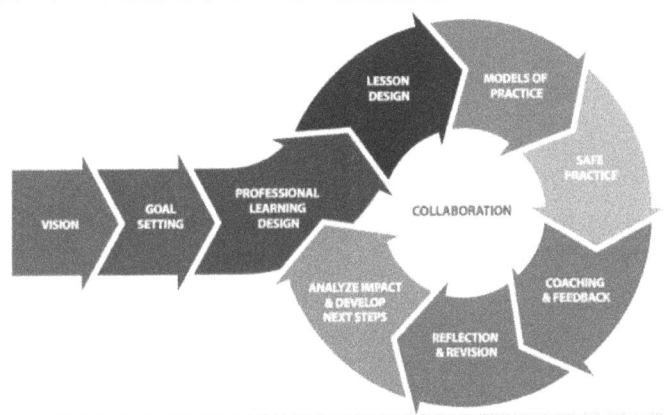

- How are teachers empowered to drive their own professional learning cycles based on their needs and the needs of the learners in their classrooms?
- How does the evidence you collect and use to guide decisions align with your vision for learners?

## A Culture of Learning and Innovation

A culture of learning must begin with a safe space for teachers to open their doors, share their practices, receive feedback, and relentlessly pursue opportunities that will enable them to more effectively develop the knowledge and skills to create the desired learning environments. Instead of using staff meetings to convey information, make time for teachers to connect and share what they are learning, risks they are taking, and what the impact of that is on their students. When innovative practices are celebrated and shared, great learning can spread through schools and the world.

If we only tell the stories of the good or gloss over the challenges, we miss the power of the learning process, instead of sharing the hurdles that are part of learning. The culture of learning and risk-taking can make great ideas and practices spread through schools and communities like wildfire, rather than keep it hidden behind closed doors.

# 7

# ACCELERATING CHANGE

Alignment in school systems is incredibly challenging. Policies created at the national, state, and local level are not organized in any coherent or logical system. Many of the policies reflect decisions that were designed for a different age. Court cases and case law establish legal precedents that in some cases have more influence than policy. Decisions are made at different levels—classrooms, schools, and school systems—and by different people who see the world from their own unique perspective. All of this ends up codified in various procedure manuals, handbooks, and informal (and yet often enduring) processes.

An example of this in California is the lasting impact of the Williams settlement from 2004, which is designed to ensure that all students in public schools have access to sufficient textbooks, adequate facilities, and qualified teachers. To ensure that schools were compliant with the textbook requirements, county offices of education were charged with the responsibility to conduct audits and physical inventories of books at some of the lowest-performing schools at that time. When we began to shift to digital resources, the practice of completing these physical inspections continued, even when it was clear that providing tablets with LTE connectivity provided access to learning resources both at school and at home. After I raised the issue of continuing this legacy practice to legislators, I was told that there was no legislative solution, since the original requirements were instituted as a result of a court case. Eventually, a joint letter from the California County Superintendents Educational Services Association and the ACLU began to clarify that digital learning materials could meet the sufficiency requirements. Nonetheless, many schools continue to operate under the understanding that a physical textbook is required for every student.

Importantly, to determine if organizational alignment exists, the vision, mission, and values should be used as the sieve to eliminate anything that runs counter to these aspirations. This should occur in all deliberations, ranging from cabinet conversations to board meetings, and should become a common practice to help create greater integrity within the system.

### Accelerator: Policy

While I have yet to find an educator who is inspired or energized by policy, the reality is that policies do have an effect on behavior and identity. Policies are in place for a number of reasons, often primarily motivated by protective factors and designed to mitigate future risk. As we made progress with personalized learning, it became evident that many of our policies were at odds with what we were hoping to achieve.

Our approach was to be inclusive and strategic in pursuing changes where we saw conflicts. Consider, for example, the rigidity of a graduation policy that may impede flexibility and learner choice.

We convened groups of students, families, staff members, and community leaders to work collaboratively to develop a "graduate profile" that transcended academic achievement. The result was a clear understanding that self-efficacy, collaboration, and problem-solving were deemed to be priorities for our learners. This graduate profile was then used in tandem with our vision, mission, and values to review our graduation policies using a collaborative process. The result was a new policy that included the graduate profile and expanded flexibility for our learners.

When we approached the culmination of this process, I learned that there had been several incomplete efforts in the past to revise the graduation policy, and that the board had previously been conflicted due to competing interests and priorities that were difficult to reconcile. After our strategic and inclusive process, we had developed enough community consensus that the policy was approved unanimously and without any dissenting speakers.

While I am of the opinion that an inclusive process is a wise way to consider policy changes, I should mention that a common error I have experienced in my career is that legal advice is often sought too late in the process. Early involvement with legal experts is a much better way to streamline the process and ensure that the outcomes are grounded in the legal realities of the educational context. For example, we engaged our legal team in the early stages of developing the Blueprint for Educational Excellence and Innovation and asked them to identify any areas of the plan that created legal or policy considerations. The early review of our draft provided us with the clarity and confidence we needed to move quickly as we shifted into implementation of the plan.

Just as we were able to benefit from legal consultation at the district level, educators at every level can often identify and experience similar opportunities by engaging their managers or supervisors, who can often help to find a way to accomplish desired goals.

## Accelerator: Technology

In addition to policy adjustments, technology can be used to accelerate—or be a drag on—the change process. For learners to have meaningful access to the world beyond their classroom, I have found it is critical to ensure that technology access is ubiquitous and equitable for all. Even in affluent environments, access to devices and connectivity will vary among students. In less affluent environments, those variations can be significant impediments for learners who are attempting to access information outside of the typical school day.

Given these variations, many policies and practices presume that learners will not have online access, and thus we resort to paper and pencil assignments, which lack flexibility and often result in longer delays in timely feedback. A more effective approach is to lean into the challenge and find solutions to ensure that all students have similar opportunities to succeed.

An inspiring example of this approach was the involvement of two of our middle schools with the Verizon Innovative Learning Schools (VILS) program. Supported by the Verizon Foundation, VILS provides devices that have built-in LTE connectivity to provide universal internet access for all learners.

When we asked students to share their experiences with the VILS program, one of the most important insights that surfaced was that the equity in access also led to improvements in students' feelings of inclusion. They felt they had access to peers and educators and could deepen relationships. Prior to having the connectivity, many learners had limited access to adult support in their homes. One student talked about how he used to feel ashamed when he would come to class unprepared, and his survival method was to act out and divert attention away from his incomplete work. With the connectivity, he felt better prepared and better able to be a productive member of the learning community. In addition to these sentiments regarding increased confidence and connectivity, program evaluations have shown reading and math scores have improved at much faster rates for students at VILS schools.

We also found success partnering with local agencies such as Computers 2 Kids, San Diego, which refurbishes donated computers and sells them at deep discounts to low-income families. Coupled with library-style checkouts of hotspots, we were able to ensure our most at-risk students had the connectivity that we felt would best support their ongoing learning.

Within the schools themselves, many learners and staff members find themselves constrained by outdated or insufficient network infrastructures that make it difficult to effectively use online resources. I recall telling our IT director, Dewayne Cossey, that I had a dream that all twenty-five thousand of our students would be able to get online at once and stream videos using our Wi-Fi system. He came back a week later with a proposal to allow for seventy-five thousand devices to access the network, with more than enough speed to accommodate abundant video streaming. When I inquired about why so many devices, he gently asked what I had in my pocket (a phone) and whether I ever used a tablet (which I did). These prompts led me to the realization that each person would likely have multiple devices online at once. Ultimately, Dewayne's plan prepared us for many contingencies and helped us to accelerate the work of building a strong wireless system throughout the district.

Another opportunity to improve the speed of change is to be mindful and strategic with respect to interoperability of both hardware and software. We informally implemented a design specification that required us to only use software that would work on any device and from anywhere. While there were a few compelling options that we declined as a result of this requirement, the speed with which we were able to adapt new devices (notably the rise of Chromebooks was prevalent during this timeframe) helped us to better serve our learners.

Similarly, data should be configured for interoperability. We were strategic in our procurement to prioritize programs that made it easier for us to push and pull data in ways that helped us to better understand the dynamic needs of learners. While this was always a work in progress, and much work remained to be done, we were moving in the direction of adaptive dashboards that pulled real-time data from multiple sources. This was possible due to the intentionality of our purchasing decisions.

Interoperability, by the way, has profound implications for learners. It is not efficient when they need to log in and log out of multiple applications, navigate multiple devices, manage an array of passwords with varied requirements, and shift attention multiple times to complete tasks. In addition to it simply being an inefficient use of time, learners will tell you that this type of disjointed experience makes it more difficult to complete projects, to remember where they stored various artifacts, and to effectively communicate with others. In an educational ecosystem, we must strive to find ways to simplify students' experiences withs technology in order to accelerate learning.

### Accelerator: Talent

People are what make the difference in social learning communities. As a result, the reality is that the majority of the money spent in education is devoted to the salaries and benefits of the people who implement the programs and services that support learners. In California, it is not uncommon for 80–90 percent of all expenses to fall into the "people" category.

People have the greatest impact on change and innovation in our schools and classrooms. However, this investment in personnel is not typically mirrored with similar levels of intentionality in recruiting, onboarding, and retaining the talent that is required to best serve our learners. Many of our systems reflect an era when employment was more stable and where teachers stayed in the profession for longer durations of time. Very few of our systems reflect the fact that we are now in a much more geographically diverse pool for the competition of talent, including the emergence of charter schools, an increasing array of private school options, online and independent school options, and certification-based programs. Lifelong learning, early education, higher education, and workforce development programs are also on the lookout for great educators.

We found that recruiting and hiring was most effective when we led with our vision, mission, and values. This served to attract those who felt resonance with our aspirations and also helped us during the hiring process to screen out those who were not aligned.

We had also inherited an archaic hiring process that had too many steps and took too long. In tandem with our union representatives, we used the collective bargaining process to refresh and streamline hiring so that we could move faster when needed and maximize our opportunities with strong candidates, who often were weighing multiple offers.

We also found that our best recruiters were current team members. When we went to job fairs, for example, our best ambassadors were employees who could speak from experience about what it was like to be a member of our team. Role-alike matchings were even more successful—having science teachers recruit new science teachers, for example, was highly effective and helped to build ownership of the hiring decisions.

Our feeling was that one of the best ways to attract and retain outstanding team members was to provide ongoing and systematic opportunities to connect and learn. That process began with the hiring mechanics itself. Vista Unified also took great pride in maintaining a vibrant Beginning Teacher Support and Assessment (BTSA) program throughout the recession of the late 2000s when hiring was slow, indicative of the high value that we placed on supporting new educators. We also did events for newly hired employees a couple of times each year, which would involve a professional learning experience along with introductions from community leaders, like the head of the Chamber of Commerce or city council representatives. These interactions were also opportunities to reinforce our vision, mission, and values.

In school systems, we also tend to underestimate the importance of positive recognition for our team members. When a survey revealed an alarming scarcity of positive feedback among our administrative team, we reconstituted our meetings to begin each one with five minutes of "compliment" time to recognize and celebrate hard work and success. We also added a "superintendent's recognition" at the beginning of each school board meeting to recognize individuals and teams that exemplified our district values of respect, trust, or collaboration. It is remarkable how these little changes can make a big difference.

Frequently, peer recognition is even more impactful than recognition from a superintendent or formal leader. At Altitude Learning, we hold weekly team gatherings (called "pulse") where peers can publicly recognize one another. It is not uncommon for peer-generated praise to elicit tears of joy, and I have seen that individuals who feel their contributions are noticed and appreciated form strong and high-performing teams. In addition, the act of complimenting others helps to create a culture of appreciative inquiry that builds on the assets and strengths that exist in all communities.

Regardless of your recognition systems, be sure to periodically pause and ensure that your approach is consistent with your stated values. As an example, recognizing individuals is sometimes inconsistent with a value of collaboration, which emphasizes the value of teams. Since no single system is perfect, using a multifaceted approach is typically the best strategy to avoid blind spots.

## The Flywheel Effect

On my first official day in the superintendent role, I hired three new principals. Due to a combination of factors, by the end of my second year on the job, twenty-four of our thirty schools had new principals. The high levels of attrition were influenced by numerous conditions, including burnout from exceptionally high workloads at the end of a long recession, which required the elimination of many positions at every level of the district or school. The first few hires were challenging for me in many respects, as I was still learning the landscape. Even more difficult was the fact that for several key positions the pool of applicants was shallow, and we had few strong candidates to consider.

In time and as a result of many changes, including our growing reputation for success and innovation, the dynamics began to shift in terms of hiring. I remember our team coming back from a job fair amazed at the long line of teaching candidates waiting to connect and learn more about how they could be a part of our district. Right before my departure, we had a vacancy for an assistant principal position and had more than three hundred applicants for the job. This was an improvement of at least ten times over the number of applications we had been receiving in my first year as superintendent. What we heard from these applicants was that they wanted to be a part of something special and that they were attracted to our vision of excellence and innovation. Additionally, the outstanding reputation of our team led many candidates to say that they wanted to connect with and learn from dedicated and talented colleagues.

When the flywheel begins moving in a positive direction with respect to the talent that exists in an organization, it has a magnetizing effect that draws in new team members who are committed and excited to be a part of the movement. As that occurs, the capacity of the organization to accelerate and improve expands, creating new and better options for our learners and for our communities.

## KEY QUESTIONS:

- How might you use accelerators such as policy, technology, and talent to gain momentum?
- How might you adjust policies in an inclusive manner to align legacy expectations with the vision for the future?
- How might technology be used to promote inclusivity and learner-centered practices?
- How might you reconsider hiring practices, onboarding, professional learning, and recognition systems to unleash the potential of the talented educators who serve learners?

Please use the hashtag #LCLeadership and share your responses on social media.

# 8

# THE FUTURE

I have often said that I was inspired to be an educator by my mom's experience as a computer teacher. On a personal level, the urgency that I feel is fueled by my experience as a dad. My own two children are growing up so quickly, and they simply don't have time for us to wait.

It feels like just yesterday that our daughter was born, and now she is driving and getting close to completing high school. Both of our kids have attended schools where I have been privileged to serve as a school leader. I wonder sometimes if I have done enough for them. I wonder sometimes if I've done enough for all of the students.

School leadership is a complex, challenging, and immensely rewarding endeavor. In my own experience, I have had many days where it seemed an overwhelming enterprise. While there will certainly be more days like that ahead, the good news is that our brightest moments are also ahead of us. We are truly on the verge of a system-wide transformation, and each of us can play a pivotal role to accelerate to models that better serve all learners. The time to lean into these opportunities is now.

This sense of urgency is fueled not only by the immediate potential to better connect with the individual strengths and interests of every learner, but also by the rapid changes in the world around us. Globalization will continue to bring us closer to the "death of distance," which provides great benefits, such as enhanced connectedness and interdependence across the world. And it also means that our youth will be competing for jobs not just with peers across town, but also with peers across the world.

For our learners, it is almost impossible to anticipate precisely how these changes will evolve over time. As a child, I certainly would not have anticipated, for example, that a mobile phone would turn into a computer connected to wireless networks. Most of us failed to anticipate how the internet would disrupt retail and advertising. And now we are talking about quantum computing and nanotechnology, which may catalyze entirely new possibilities.

Learner-centered leadership is a mindset. It is not a title or role within an organization. Each of us, whether we are teachers, assistant principals, assistant superintendents, board members, or community collaborators, holds the potential to make a difference in the lives of our learners. In fact, it will take all of us to make the changes necessary to build the brightest future possible. We are on the verge. Let me tell you why.

The good news here is that organizations that were once modeled on the industrial-age model of hierarchies and stability are reconstituting to become more adaptive. In his incredible book *Reinventing Organizations: A Guide to Creating Organizations Inspired by the Next Stage of Human Consciousness*, Frederic Laloux describes how "the organizations we have invented were tied to the prevailing worldview and consciousness," and he outlines how organizations have evolved from egocentric → ethnocentric → world-centric → pluralistic → authentic perspectives over time. Laloux is clear that each paradigm both transcends and includes the previous one.

Organizations are evolving to shift from command and control, predictable and narrowly defined outcomes to ones that focus on relationships, on organizational culture, and on service to the world. In these new organizations, according to Laloux, "members of the organization are invited to listen in and understand what the organization wants to become, what purpose it wants to serve," where teams lean into opportunities to self-organize and thrive. In these evolved settings, shared values are the consistent reference to provide coherence in a rapidly changing context. School systems have an opportunity to learn from new models and to create more adaptive systems, as well.

## Imagining the School as a Start-Up

The stability of the public education system is apparent in numerous policies and procedures that are designed to codify practices and establish boundaries. The multilayered, participative structures of advisory committees and open governance of school boards are both a stabilizing component and also a representation of the desire to ensure inclusivity. Transparency laws are another mechanism to ensure that community members have access to information regarding process, and increased accountability measures ensure that outcomes are similarly available to the public.

In contrast to the rigid hierarchies of public school systems, start-ups embody the "flat organization," in which performance is more important than status. Open office concepts, informal attire, and other nudges to promote frequent interactions among employees are all intentional shifts to ensure that the focus is on productivity. The lack of "authority" empowers every team member to assume responsibility for his or her own actions, and a highly visible performance framework ensures that there is clarity around goals, outcomes, and initiatives.

When I consider what I would do differently in the role of superintendent after having experienced a start-up culture, several key actions come to mind:

1. Reconfigure space to promote openness, flexibility, and virtual collaboration
2. Model informal attire
3. Shift from annual to quarterly time horizons

I would enact these changes with the adults in the system as well as students, in order to better prepare them for success outside of school. The first two actions focus on extending collaboration, which is essential in developing the social-emotional habits and skills that students will require to thrive in our rapidly changing world. The last is an interesting way to shift away from the annual, agricultural cycle that we currently inhabit in education toward a faster, more iterative model that is better aligned with brain research, as well as with the rhythms of the workforce.

There are clear benefits and disadvantages in each of these organizational approaches. The tradeoff for inclusion in a public school setting is that the pace of change is very slow. As technology and other forces such as globalization are accelerating the rate of change outside of schools, the gap between the reality within schools and outside of them creates severe risks for learners, in that they will be unprepared for life beyond their educational experience. With that said, the tradeoff for the speed of start-ups is that the less-inclusive, more distributed decision-making process allows for wider variation in the quality of those decisions. In some cases, that results in great insights and innovations, but the risks of more significant failure are also increased.

My vision for the future is that we should combine the best of both of these worlds to better serve our learners. Innovative start-ups that move quickly have the ability to adapt and partner with public school systems that embody community inclusivity. This collaboration is a great model for magnifying our relative strengths and mitigating our risks. Just as collaboration is essential for young learners, adults can lean into their opportunities to deepen relationships and learn from one another.

## The Learner-Centered Movement

There is a movement underway right now. In my current role as the chief impact officer at Altitude Learning, I have had the opportunity to visit hundreds of schools across the country, and I see strong examples of learner-centric practices emerging in all types of schools and in all geographic settings. I have observed learner-centric practices in schools like Punahou in Hawaii, and at Phillips Academy Andover near Boston. I have also seen them in charter schools like Rocketship in San Jose and CICS West Belden in Chicago. They are also evident in districts like Lindsay Unified in central California, Franklin West Supervisory Union in Vermont, and Kettle Moraine in Wisconsin. While the backdrop varies and the entry points for learner-centric practices are also distinct, the experience of the learner in these innovative environments is one where they know themselves and see their place in the world. They see themselves as changemakers. They are highly engaged, and they are inspired.

At Punahou, learners have the opportunity to engage with a faculty advisor who can help them to work on a "passion project," and the advisor then works with teams of other educators who help the learner create and implement a custom plan for their learning. At Rocketship and in Lindsay Unified, learners can clearly articulate their learning goals and describe how they will prioritize their time to achieve those outcomes. In Franklin West, learners can demonstrate proficiency tied to academic outcomes and social-emotional learning competencies and can receive credit for those learning experiences, even if they occurred outside of the formal context of school. These are all examples of learner agency, personalized learning, competency-based education, and open-walled experiences.

KM Global, Kettle Moraine School District, Wisconsin, October 2018

The photo from KM Global, one of the schools-within-a-school in Kettle Moraine School District in Wisconsin, is a great example of what you see at places where learner-centric practices are evident. Overt levels of student engagement are apparent. Learners are frequently in small groups working collaboratively with one another. In this photo, you also see an educator meeting individually with a student (left side of the photo, on the couch), having a conversation with the learner about progress related to their individual goals.

Here's the thing to remember about these examples: they are happening anywhere and everywhere. There is nothing inherently unique about Vista or Lindsay, other than that they share common commitments to be responsive to their learners, and they have gone about the change process in a way that involves the community. These practices are replicable. Any school and any district has the capacity to make the same change. Now we know how.

## Call to Action

Primarily, what is necessary is a bias to action. The time is now. If it isn't now, when will the right moment come? We are the ones. If we are not the ones, then who is?

I sometimes hear that the path forward is too uncertain and full of risk. A better approach is to consider the risks of inaction in comparison to the risks of moving forward. All too often, we forget that the risks of inaction are known, and, in my view, they are unacceptable. It is unacceptable to have almost 20 percent of our learners fail to graduate from high school. It is unacceptable to have increasing levels of disengagement as learners matriculate through our system. It is unacceptable that the unique strengths and interests of each learner are ignored, leading our learners to feel that schools are irrelevant. It is unacceptable that learners from different cultural backgrounds feel invisible.

And just as a thought exercise, let's play forward what happens to us as a society if we continue with the status quo. Continuation of the factory model of teaching and learning implies that we condition our youth to be told what to do, when to do it, and how to do it. Even the learners that "succeed" in this model will likely fail in a world of work and a landscape of civic engagement that requires self-direction, high levels of collaboration, and the ability to find and solve complex problems. Companies and organizations are already evolving in the direction of values-based, self-organized teams. Citizenship will also require us to be critical thinkers with the capacity to form coalitions and address emergent challenges and opportunities.

In an age where technology and globalization will create competition across the world, young people who are waiting to be told what to do will be at a massive disadvantage if others have been better prepared for the landscape ahead by having developed habits and skills to show initiative.

Maintaining the industrial-age model of schooling in a post-industrial era makes no sense. It does a disservice to our learners, to our families, to our communities, and to society.

Now is the time for us to act.

### Plan-Do-Study-Act

While the path forward is still uncertain, trailblazers have set a path that can now be followed to move faster and with greater likelihood of success. As we move, we need to learn from improvement science and implement ongoing cycles of "Plan-Do-Study-Act," and be prepared for ongoing adjustments.

In the "plan" stage, the foundation is the will to act. Once that is in place, the leader should take stock of the following:

1. Is there a clear understanding among all stakeholders of the Framework for the Future? Is there a clear vision, mission, and values? Are there measurable goals and an aligned set of roles and responsibilities in place? Do you have a plan that includes strategies, actions, and resource allocations that are also aligned?
2. Is there a clear understanding that relational trust and social capital are foundational in the success of the changes ahead? Is there a clear understanding of the strategy that has been identified for the changes ahead (i.e., where in the Rogers curve will you begin and then extend the change)?
3. Is there a clear learning model that serves as a framework for the work ahead? Is there a guiding coalition in place to navigate the complexities of the change process?
4. Are the accelerators in place to set the foundation for scaling with quality and sustaining the movement? Have you aligned policy, technology, and talent to optimize for the desired future state? If not yet, do you have a timeline and plan to align on the way?

After ensuring readiness, it is time to get into the hard work of the change itself. This is the "do" stage that is typified by rapid activity. We've seen these changes take root in hundred-year-old school districts like Vista Unified and in start-up independent schools, such as AltSchool. Arcadia Unified was able to move from concept to opening a new lab school in three months by embracing the mindset of acting like a start-up. Leaders across the nation are taking the initiative and moving to learner-centered models. In my mind, it is far better for us as educators to lead the way than to expect an outside-in approach to result in the changes that are needed.

Almost in parallel with the orientation to action and the critical nature of the "do" activities is the integral imperative to "study," then "act" to make adjustments. None of us has all of the answers. The transformation ahead is an adaptive challenge that is best navigated in community, and in the constant mode of co-construction. Connectedness, both internal to an organization and to the external world, is essential for ongoing learning. This is true for our learners, for our educators, and for families and community members, as well. Building systems and procedures to promote internal connectedness is imperative. Reaching out to early adopters is a great strategy to accelerate the journey. It is in community that we can step back, reflect, and determine necessary adjustments. It is in community that we create the capacity to address emergent challenges. It is in community that we transform.

Along the way, each of us must remember that our role is to be in service to others. This is not heroism. Anyone can serve. Paying forward the lessons learned along the way is not only beneficial from the perspective of self-reflection but also models the mindset that will be necessary for us to make the collective jump to new learning models. Stephen Covey articulated this as a "maturity continuum," where we move from dependence to independence to interdependence. That can also be thought of as a shift from an egocentrism to sociocentrism. It is the shift from "me" to "we."

We should remember that the rationale for an egocentric or independent mindset is rooted in resource scarcity and tied to our very real need for survival. When resources are limited and individual sustainability is tied to a person's ability to secure those resources, that compels a competitive mindset where there are winners and losers.

In game theory, this type of model is known as a "zero sum" activity because the net result when there are winners and losers is that there are no overall gains for the community. The classic example here would be a game of checkers, where for every winner there must necessarily be a loser. If you kept a tally of the winners and losers and then netted the difference, it would also be zero. In this setting, there is no benefit to helping your "opponent."

In the world of the future, resource scarcity is no longer our reality. As a society, we have gone from the team of individuals and tribes of hunters and gatherers to more complex models where we exchange goods and services to maximize the benefits of efficient models of food production. In the words of Daniel Pink in his book *A Whole New Mind*, we are also in an age of abundance where material goods are so easily and rapidly produced that our challenges shift to the management of surpluses. If you doubt this reality, just think about the recent rise of the self-storage industry and the increasing emphasis on minimalism as a counterbalance.

Given continued improvements in technology, the future will also make computational thinking increasingly free. Given the way that information networks function, there are legitimate and meaningful compounding effects on the horizon, and the sharing of ideas and information can provide dramatic benefits on a wide scale.

The overall result of these improvements is that we are approaching a time where "non-zero" is the future. Instead of clear winners and losers, our inherent interdependence will be more clear, and we will shift to more of a collaborative orientation. We have been moving in this direction for many years, documented through treaties and trade organizations, overall reductions in international wars, and even through concepts such as open-source development.

Learner-centered leaders must model this shift to openness and collaboration.

## Metacompetency

The guiding reference, or "true north," along the journey is to see lifelong learning as *the* metacompetency. There are numerous building blocks to achieve that metacompetency, including a strong sense of self and an ongoing spirit of possibility as a changemaker who is driving to have a positive impact on the world. Learner-centered frameworks help to guide the way forward and identify key elements to help our learners develop the knowledge, skills, and habits that will be required to collaboratively solve emerging and complex real-world challenges.

Developing this human capacity to learn will be incredibly important as technology continues to advance. Advances in computing will provide us with unprecedented opportunities to decide how to leverage resources for the benefit of individuals, society, and our planet. Just as learning needs to be in the foreground in our schools, with technology in the background, we must remember that technology is not a direct replacement for people. In its proper conception, technology is an enablement to make people better.

In a learner-centric system, the educator is in service to the learner. The leader is in service to the learner. And, technology is in service to the learner. In this way, educators, leaders, and technology are enablements to our young people. We must remember that this is the right and proper sequence. It is unwise and potentially very dangerous for us to reverse the model to place us in service to the technology. We are at a critical stage in our development where it will be up to us and to the next generation to ensure that we stay grounded in our humanity.

## Forward Together

The future is unknown and rapidly changing. There is no way that a prescriptive approach will be the right one. Education is also complex. Great learning is messy. Kids are different. Community and context matters. Oversimplification is a major mistake.

And yet, we know that the risks of maintaining our current model are too high. The way forward is together. The time is now.

Let's embrace a plan-do-study-act model and work together to do what is necessary to connect with our learners, to ignite their passion for learning, and to help them to have a foundation for lifelong learning. Let's be sure that they have the knowledge, habits, and skills to solve complex problems in collaboration with one another. Let's be sure that *all* learners have the opportunity to experience the best education possible. And let's model the way, working in collaborative communities to expand opportunities for the future. Our kids need it. The world needs us—each of us—to step up and lead the way.

I end most of my talks the same way, which is to refer to two questions that Margaret Wheatley posits are central for any leader: 1) Who cares? And, 2) What is possible here?

Who cares about our kids and our future? It turns out that just about everybody does. Invite them to be a part of the journey. Be assertive in inviting our learners to be involved at every step of the process.

What is possible here? After convening people who care, invite them to explore possibilities and to avoid the paralysis of focusing on the very real challenges and obstacles. Leaders embrace an optimistic view of the future, and by asking others to dream, we expand horizons and create new potential.

What is possible here is that we can influence the present and we can shape the future. By staying focused on learners and learning and by working together, we can make a profound and positive difference in the lives of individuals, in the vitality of communities, and on society as a whole. That is the purpose of education. In service to others, it is also our purpose as individuals.

I invite you to join us on the journey. Let's do this together. Let's do it now.

# ACKNOWLEDGMENTS

There are so many influential people who have contributed to my leadership journey and to this book.

I should begin with my parents, Margaret and Milan, and my siblings, Lenka and Paul. Coming from a family of thoughtful changemakers has been a tremendous gift in my life. This definitely includes all of my aunts, uncles, cousins, and extended family. Special thanks to Chuck and Sharon Patterson and to Charlie Patterson for providing a home and a second family for me as a child.

Special thanks to my leadership mentors in my teen years and early twenties. Some names that stand out for me are Chris Owen from Nevada Union High School, Angie Chrisman from UC Santa Cruz, and Diane Agliam from Glenwood Elementary. To the Pepperdine faculty and team who encouraged me to take a relational approach to leadership, I am eternally grateful. Special thanks to Dr. Bob Paull, Dr. Linda Purrington, and Dr. Margaret Riel.

Thanks to the amazing people from Carlsbad Unified who provided me with such incredible opportunities. I was very fortunate to learn from Cheryl Ernst, Dr. John Roach, Dr. Susan Bentley, Gaylen Freeman, Walter Freeman, Steve Maddox, Suzanne O'Connell, and Torrie Norton. To all of the incredible directors, coordinators, principals, assistant principals, teachers, and classified staff who were my colleagues on the way, I am so fortunate to have been able to work with you and learn from you.

Thanks to the school board in Vista for taking a chance on a youthful, first-time superintendent. Your courage and relentless focus on students set an incredible example and fortified the entire community. The visionary board members that I had the privilege of working with are Dr. Steve Lily, Rich Alderson, Carol Herrera, Elizabeth Jaka, Angela Chunka, Jim Gibson, Cipriano Vargas, and Rosemary Smithfield.

Thanks to the unbelievably talented and dedicated cabinet in Vista. We had a dream team, and your contributions are appreciated. I was incredibly fortunate. Thank you, Jeanie Luckey, Myrna Vallely, Donna Caperton, Matt Doyle, Brett Killeen, Sherry Opacic, and Elaine Alexandres. To all of the admin team in Vista, I am incredibly grateful. Special appreciation to Raylene Veloz and to Michelle Bell for your support. Thank you for your steadfast focus on our students.

Thanks to all of the teachers, educators, and leaders in Vista. There are too many to name here. I hope that this book puts a spotlight on your heroic work. For the families and community in Vista, thank you for your trust and confidence in our team. And for the students, thank you for inspiring us. Your brilliance is already changing the world for the better, and the best days are ahead.

Thanks to the team from Altitude Learning (formerly AltSchool). Thanks to Max Ventilla, Bharat Mediratta, and Coddy Johnson for encouraging me to take the leap into the challenge of supporting many communities. I am also grateful to the amazing team and especially thankful to Colleen Broderick and Sam Franklin for their inspiring leadership. I appreciate those who directly encouraged this project, including Ben Kornell, Eve Wachtell, Maggie Quale, and Andrea Helling. Thanks also to Sandy Cima and Emily Amata for their tireless support.

To my colleagues who are superintendents, I applaud your leadership and I hope that you know how much you continue to inspire

## ACKNOWLEDGMENTS

me. Special thanks to the incredible superintendents in San Diego County and to my colleagues in the League of Innovative Schools.

Thanks, also, to those who have taken on informal mentoring roles in my development. Karen Cator, Myron Rogers, Yong Zhao, Andy Calkins, and many others have taken the time and the interest to cultivate and nurture my ongoing learning, and I am so grateful for their support.

Thank you to all the incredible leaders from TICAL and ACSA who have modeled a learner-centered approach throughout my career. To Rowland Baker and Michael Simkins, who saw something in me as a very young administrator—your trust in me opened up many opportunities for learning, and I am very grateful for your servant leadership. Special thanks to Lisa Gonzales, who was my earliest writing partner, conference co-presenter, and a constant source of inspiration and encouragement.

To all who have made transitions with me from one place to another, I am incredibly humbled by your confidence. Special thanks to Catina Hancock, who has been with me on every step of the journey. She is a relational leader who has helped to keep me grounded, while also working tirelessly to achieve a vision of a better future for all learners.

And thanks to Katie Martin, who was my primary source of encouragement and support for this book project. Her example and her commitment to provide ideas, feedback, and coaching along the way were instrumental in this process. Simply put, without Katie, this book would not exist. Thanks for encouraging me to be vulnerable and to share my perspective in the hopes that it serves to help others.

Finally, thank you to Nicole, Alexandria, and Coltrane. You are my everything.

# ABOUT THE AUTHOR

Devin Vodicka is recognized as one of the most innovative educational leaders in the country. A multi-time California Superintendent of the Year, he was a frequent collaborator with the Department of Education's Office of Educational Technology under President Obama and was heavily involved with the Digital Promise League of Innovative Schools.

Devin is renowned for his unique understanding of how technology can help transform learning, most notably how learner-centered models can play a catalytic role in enabling educators to better support each student's progress and success. During his five-year tenure as superintendent of Vista Unified School District, Devin led his twenty-five-thousand-student community through districtwide changes that resulted in major improvements across every academic and behavioral metric, from college readiness to truancy. Devin currently serves as the chief impact officer at San Francisco-based Altitude Learning, which is supporting schools across the country with training and technology in the shift to learner-centered education models. He lives in San Diego with his wife and two children.

# MORE FROM IMPRESS BOOKS

*Empower*
What Happens When Students Own Their Learning
**By A.J. Juliani and John Spencer**

In an ever-changing world, educators and parents must take a role in helping students prepare themselves for *anything*. That means unleashing their creative potential! In **Empower,** **A.J. Juliani** and **John Spencer** provide teachers, coaches, and administrators with a roadmap that will inspire innovation, authentic learning experiences, and practical ways to empower students to pursue their passions while in school.

*Learner-Centered Innovation*
Spark Curiosity, Ignite Passion, and Unleash Genius
Katie Martin

Learning opportunities and teaching methods *must* evolve to match the ever-changing needs of today's learners. In **Learner-Centered Innovation, Katie Martin** offers insights into how to make the necessary shifts and create an environment where learners at every level are empowered to take risks in pursuit of learning and growth rather than perfection.

***Unleash Talent***
*Bringing Out the Best in Yourself and the Learners You Serve*
Kara Knollmeyer

In **Unleash Talent**, educator and principal **Kara Knollmeyer** explains that by exploring the core elements of talent—passion, skills, and personality traits—you can uncover your gifts and help others do the same. Whether you are a teacher, administrator, or custodian, this insightful guide will empower you to use your unique talents to make a powerful impact on your school community.

***Reclaiming Our Calling***
*Hold on to the Heart, Mind, and Hope of Education*
Brad Gustafson

Children are more than numbers, and we are called to teach and reach them accordingly. In this genre-busting book, award-winning educator and principal **Brad Gustafson** uses stories to capture the heart, mind, and hope of education.

***Take the L.E.A.P***
*Ignite a Culture of Innovation*
By Elisabeth Bostwick

**Take the L.E.A.P.: Ignite a Culture of Innovation** will inspire and support you as you to take steps to grow beyond traditional and self-imposed boundaries. Award-winning educator **Elisabeth Bostwick** shares stories and practical strategies to help you challenge conventional thinking and create the conditions that empower meaningful learning.

MORE FROM IMPRESS BOOKS

***Drawn to Teach***
*An Illustrated Guide to Transforming Your Teaching*
Written by Josh Stumpenhorst, Illustrated by Trevor Guthke

If you're looking for ways to help your students succeed, you won't find the answer in gimmicks, trends, or fads. Great teaching isn't about test results or data; it's about connecting with students and empowering them to own their learning. Through this clever, illustrated guide, **Josh Stumpenhorst** reveals the key characteristics all top educators share in common and shows you how to implement them in your teaching practice.

***Math Recess***
*Playful Learning in an Age of Disruption*
By Sunil Singh and Dr. Christopher Brownell

In the theme of recess, where a treasure chest of balls, ropes, and toys would be kept for children to play with, this book holds a deep and imaginative collection of fun mathematical ideas, puzzles, and problems. Written for anyone interested in or actively engaged in schools—parents, teachers, administrators, school board members—this book shows math as a playful, fun, and wonderfully human activity that everyone can enjoy… for a lifetime!

***Innovate Inside the Box***
*Empowering Learners Through UDL and Innovator's Mindset*

In *Innovate Inside the Box,* George Couros and Katie Novak provide informed insight on creating purposeful learning opportunities for all students. By combining the power of the Innovator's Mindset and Universal Design for Learning (UDL), they empower educators to create opportunities that will benefit every learner.

***Personal & Authentic***
*Designing Learning Experiences That Impact a Lifetime*
By Thomas C. Murray

In **Personal & Authentic**, **Thomas C. Murray** reveals the power of designing awe-inspiring experiences that are grounded in relationships and learner-centered by design. Inherently relevant and contextualized, it is this kind of learning that lasts a lifetime.